Living on Tiptoe

LIVING ON TIPTOE

The Healing Power of Love

T. Cecil Myers

A Key-Word Book
WORD BOOKS, PUBLISHER
Waco, Texas

First Key-Word edition: March 1978

LIVING ON TIPTOE
Copyright © 1972 by Word, Incorporated, Waco, Texas 76703.

All rights reserved. No part of this book may be reproduced in any form except for brief quotations in reviews without written permission from the publisher.

ISBN 0-8499-4104-0
Library of Congress catalog card number: 72-84166
Printed in the United States of America

Quotations from the Revised Standard Version of the Bible, copyright 1946 and 1952, © 1971, 1973 by the Division of Christian Education of the National Council of the Churches of Christ in the United States of America, used by permission; the Today's English Version of the New Testament, copyright © American Bible Society, 1966; *The New English Bible* © The Delegates of The Oxford University Press, 1961, 1970, reprinted by permission; *The New Testament in Modern English* by J. B. Phillips, © J. B. Phillips 1958, 1960, 1972. All Scripture quotations are identified in the text by name of translator or abbreviations in conventional form.

The quotation on p. 51 is from "The Laws of God, the Laws of Man" from The Collected Poems of A. E. Housman. Copyright 1922 by Holt, Rinehart and Winston, Inc. Copyright 1950 by Barclays Bank Ltd. Reprinted by permission of Holt, Rinehart and Winston, Inc.

*To the congregations of
Brookhaven, Trinity, Sam Jones, Grace, and Athens
First United Methodist Churches,
whose love and encouragement
have provided an atmosphere
in which the healing powers
could work in many people*

Contents

Introduction • 9

1. God Wills Wholeness • 11
2. Incurable—Man's Term, Not God's • 19
3. You Need Not Stay the Way You Are! • 28
4. Healing and Forgiveness • 36
5. Learning to Face Up to Life • 42
6. Forget Yourself into Usefulness • 54
7. Learn to Accept What You Cannot Change • 62
8. Change Your Attitudes and You Change Your Life • 70
9. The Dull Monotony of Over and Over and How It Is Healed • 79
10. The Healing Power of Hope • 87
11. On Loving Yourself the Right Way • 96
12. Ten Tests for Emotional Health • 106

Introduction

Religion, medicine, and psychology are not in competition. They complement each other. One of the major challenges in the area of health is that group that has no organic diseases. A dentist asked an elderly woman who was always complaining if she had ever been real sick. "No," replied the patient, "but then I've never been real well either." Some people never get well. The elder brother (Luke 15) for all practical purposes left home when the younger brother was born. He never came back. His behavior at the return of a lost younger brother was the outcropping of jealousy and a sense of rejection. Never understanding the scope of the father's love, he remained sick. It is not enough to heal the body. In fact, the body cannot be completely whole unless there is health of mind and spirit. Sick souls and sick minds make for sick bodies.

In the United States we have made enormous strides in medicine. The great problems of health are shifting to the emotional-spiritual field. We now understand that scientific medicine alone is insufficient to meet the growing tide of emotionally induced problems that counselors, doctors, and ministers encounter daily.

Many illnesses could be prevented by choice. Even

after an illness is well under way, the choice of attitude and the quality of the inner life may have great bearings on arrest or cure of a disease. We may have the choice of health, chronic illness, or even death.

These chapters are offered with the hope that the healing power of God may be brought to bear upon the lives of persons suffering from the stresses, strains, and illnesses of life. There are destructive forces at work in the world. And there are healing forces that can be used to enable us to live on tiptoe.

Jesus said pointedly, "Heal the sick!" As a minister I feel that is one of my functions. I cooperate with doctors and psychiatrists in every way, believing that God uses many vessels to bring wholeness. I believe he uses what we call miracles to make people well. He wills health. My prayer for you is that you be well in soul, body, and mind.

I am indebted to Mrs. Harold E. Braswell for her competent services in preparing the manuscript. Ideas and illustrations have come from many sources. For all who have helped I am grateful.

You can be whole. God wills it. I promise it.

CECIL MYERS

First United Methodist Church
Athens, Georgia

1

God Wills Wholeness

IT IS THE WILL OF GOD that we be whole, sane, healthy, radiant persons. There are those who seem to believe that sickness, death, feeling depressed are the will of God and that it takes a certain amount of suffering to make a saint. That is not true. A person may use his suffering and become a saint, or he may handle his suffering beautifully because he is a saint. Take a piece of paper, and write a list of things that your child could do that are bad enough for you to punish him with cancer or heart trouble or tuberculosis or arthritis. Would you do that to your child? No!

God does not will sickness or failure or suffering or death. We suffer because the laws of God operate for all, because of our interdependence, because of our ignorance, because of our willful choices. I agree with Dr. Paul Tournier when he said that sickness "can destroy all man's values, and as a doctor I shall not cease to try to snatch its victims from it."[1]

Frequently when we speak of the will of God, some dark, distasteful thing comes to mind. Many times I have stood by the bedside of a dying child, or a sick patient; I have worked with families to secure hospitalization for a mentally ill person; I have watched a loved family member writhe in pain on the bed. I have heard people say, "This is God's will!" I always want to shout "No! God isn't like that!"

One of the dearest little boys I ever knew began to be listless and inactive. This was unusual for this six-year-old. Examination revealed widespread cancer that seemed to center in the lower spine. For weeks he was in the hospital. He suffered a great deal, then lapsed into a coma and was gone. I held his hand as the end came. As the father held the boy's mother in his arms, I heard her say, "It is God's will. He needed him for his flower garden." I searched for words to tell them this was not God's will, but that God could use what he did not choose, and over several weeks helped them to see the truth.

Some of my minister friends say, "If it helps them to believe that, let them." But there is no final comfort in a lie. If it is God's will that men be crippled, deformed, stunted in mind, pale, anemic, then giving money to heart funds, polio drives, the maintenance of hospitals and convalescent homes is sinful and is an affront to God's will.

Paul asked, "Shall we continue in sin that grace may abound?" Then he replied, "God forbid!" I believe that God wills wholeness, health, sanity, success, and peace. To call sickness, war, or mental illness the will of God is a far greater blasphemy than to deny the virgin birth, or the Trinity, or any other cherished belief of the Christian faith.

The will of God is when two people in love stand before the altar in commitment to God and one another "till death do us part." Or when parents stand at an altar and dedicate a lovely baby to God. Or when a home is dedicated to the glory of God and the service of man. Or when we succeed in business, or

God Wills Wholeness

practice truth, love, compassion in our relationships with people, or give ourselves in service to man to lift the level of living where we are. Or when we are well and strong of mind and body, in full bloom of thought and action. This is the intentional will of God.

We are created for health. I believe there is a strong force in us that maintains health, that works for our recovery when we are sick. We most certainly become sick when negative emotions block the healing force. Such emotions as fear, guilt, hate, greed, pain, loneliness, and boredom are negative and produce illness. But over against these is another force that works to maintain health and to restore it once it is lost.

The healing ministry of Jesus occupies the largest place in the four Gospels. Except for the accounts of the last week in Jesus' life, there is more about healing than all else. There are nineteen major acts of healing and several lesser ones. Here is one of them:

> One sabbath when he went to dine at the house of a ruler who belonged to the Pharisees, they were watching him. And behold, there was a man before him who had dropsy. And Jesus spoke to the lawyers and Pharisees, saying, "Is it lawful to heal on the sabbath, or not?" But they were silent. Then he took him and healed him, and let him go. And he said to them, "Which of you, having an ass or an ox that has fallen into a well, will not immediately pull him out on a sabbath day?" And they could not reply to this. (Luke 14:1–6, RSV)

The mere healing of the body was never Jesus' intention. He asked the man at the pool, "Do you want to be made whole?" To the Syrophoenecian woman he said, "Daughter, your faith has made you whole." To another he said, "Sin no more lest a worse thing come upon you." Jesus was concerned with wholeness: mind, spirit, body.

We look on these acts as miracles. They are not miracles in that Jesus broke the laws of the universe. God does not do that. Dr. Weatherhead has defined a miracle this way: ". . . a law abiding event by which God accomplishes his redemptive purposes through the release of energies which belong to a higher plane of being than any with which we are normally familiar."[2] Jesus simply moved on a higher plane than we yet understand, but it is a plane of thought and will available to every man who has faith! Healing to Jesus was an expression of God's natural law, a calling into play of laws and forces that we have not yet discovered. The divinity of Christ does not imply that he suspended the laws of the universe. He used them. Furthermore, he didn't perform his healing acts to prove his divinity. He himself was proof enough!

Unfortunately, after the first few years of the Christian era, the church began to lose interest in healing. From A.D. 300 to 1800 there was little interest in it. This is difficult to understand since Jesus sent his followers out to preach, baptize, *and heal.* "Then he called his twelve disciples to him and gave them authority to cast out unclean spirits and to cure every kind of ailment and disease" (Matt. 10:1, NEB).

There are seven major instances of healing in the Book of Acts. But the church soon began to neglect this aspect of her ministry. We have preached and baptized, but we have not gone all the way with Jesus' injunction. Dr. Paul Tillich in his book *The*

God Wills Wholeness

New Being wrote: "The gospels, certainly, are not responsible for this disappearance of power in the picture of Jesus. . . . but, we are responsible, ministers, laymen, theologians, who forgot that 'savior' means 'healer,' he who makes whole and sane what is broken and insane, in mind and body."[3] Gradually, the idea arose that God had withdrawn his healing power and that men had to bear their suffering as Christ bore his cross and that sickness was punishment for sin. St. Cyprian put it bluntly, "The sins of Christians have weakened the power of the church."[4] We have lost the power to heal, not because God has withdrawn it, but because we have hidden it under a pile of administrative detail, emphasis on bigness, success, and material things in the church.

Our world is sick. Hospitals are filled, mental facilities are taxed to the limit, hospitals for alcoholics are bulging at the seams. Millions of people walk the streets half alive. Millions are addicted to dope, liquor, or some habit that threatens to destroy them. They search for wholeness in ways it cannot be found. But so many people suffer who do not need to, and multitudes more die long before their time.

It is estimated that only 25 percent of illness is organic. Seventy-five percent is functional. This means that three of four people who see doctors have nothing wrong organically, but something keeps their organs from functioning properly. They need to get themselves straightened out inside. A doctor admitted recently that most of his patients do not need his pills.

Illness is rampant across the earth in a wide variety of forms: physical, emotional, mental, spiritual. Much of this illness is outside the traditional work area of the medical doctor. If we can lay hold on the truth that there is a healing force working in us to maintain health and to restore it when we are sick, and if we can learn to cooperate with this force, then much illness will disappear, and we will be healthier, happier, and more useful people. This force is familiar to every doctor. He calls it nature. I prefer to call it the healing force or power of God. To the discovery and use of that healing force this book is dedicated.

No tissue of the human body is wholly removed from the influence of the spirit. For relief of our illnesses we need another kind of doctor and medicine. Dr. Paul Tillich wrote:

> . . . faith means being grasped by a power that is greater than we are, a power that shakes us and turns us, and transforms us and heals us. Surrender to this power is faith. The people whom Jesus could heal and can heal are those who did and do this self-surrender to the healing power in him. They surrender their persons, split, contradicting themselves, disgusted and despairing about themselves, hateful of themselves, and therefore hostile towards everybody else; afraid of life, burdened with guilt feelings, accusing and excusing themselves, fleeing from others into loneliness, fleeing from themselves to others, trying finally to escape from the threats of existence into the painful and deceptive safety of mental and bodily disease. As such beings they surrender to Jesus and this surrender is what we call faith![5]

One of the clearest things about Jesus is the impression of his inexhaustible power. He did not claim to be the power, only the channel. "The Father that dwelleth in me, he doeth the works," said Jesus (John 14:10). That same power is available for healing today. But we have become so worldly wise, so

God Wills Wholeness 17

scientific, so sophisticated that we are blind and deaf to the great movements of the Spirit of God. We do not give him a chance to bring wholeness in us even though God has provided enough power within his laws to do all that is in accord with his will. The higher order breaks in upon us from time to time in the healing and transforming of people and we call it a miracle. Actually it is what God wills for us all the time. He wills wholeness. There are some diseases that must await their healing beyond death, but that is a part of life. When physical healing isn't possible, soul healing is, and our spirits can be so transformed that sickness and death are transformed into glory. God's will is wholeness.

I want to share some steps with you in healing. These have validity for our own emotional, spiritual, mental, physical healing, and the healing of those we love. Think of them, follow them through, use them.

Relax—body, mind, spirit. God's spirit has difficulty penetrating the tensed-up body, the closed mind, the doubting spirit. Read Isaiah 40 and Psalm 23.

Meditate on the reality and power of God. Say over and over, "God wills wholeness and God can give wholeness!" Read 2 Timothy 1:7 and Luke 12:27–31.

Ask for removal of all that is sinful, wrong, negative. Ask for removal of unbelief. Ask to be clean, utterly forgiven of all that estranges from God and one's best self. Read Psalm 51 and Luke 15.

Ask for God's love and power in your life. Never be ashamed to ask God for what you really want. Read James 4 and Philippians 6:4.

Use every means available to you in healing: the competent doctor, medicines, hospitals, the latest methods in therapy. God works through people to perform his miracles. Read Luke 11:9–13.

See yourself or your loved one as well and whole, rid of whatever infirmities keep you from being what God wills and what you want. Read Matthew 8:5–17.

Thank God for hearing your prayer and for healing you and for an increase in love and power within you. Read Psalm 103:1–5.

Share your faith in the greatness and goodness of God with at least one other person. Read Acts 20:32–35.

God wills wholeness!

2

Incurable—
Man's Term, Not God's

SEVERAL YEARS AGO I was visiting in a hospital, and a doctor asked me to step into a room and see a patient with him. When I asked why, my friend said that a few years ago the man had a gastric ulcer, was hospitalized and operated upon. The ulcer was removed, and the man was soon discharged from the hospital. But instead of getting well, he soon developed another ulcer and was now back in the hospital, awaiting surgery.

We went into the room, the doctor introduced me, and then excused himself. In the course of our conversation I discovered that when the first operation had been performed no one had talked with the man about causes, nothing had been said about his fears. No one showed any real concern about his soul. Even though he was a church member, he had not called his pastor.

As we talked, I discovered that the ulcer was not his problem at all. He had a nagging wife who was not satisfied with his income. She was always taunting him about their social position—comparing him with his classmates in school and telling him that he had failed her and the children. His only reaction to her constant tirades was ulcers.

When I pointed this out, he saw what was happening to him. Then he suggested prayer. I laid my hands on his head and prayed for wholeness, healing of body, mind, spirit.

The doctor went on with the surgery. But he said he had never seen such a rapid recovery in all of his experience. In a conversation with his wife, I told her what was happening, and for the first time she realized what was happening. We prayed together for wholeness. Now that family is a happy one, the children are in college, the husband is successful in his relationships, and the wife has gotten her values straight.

We began by saying that God wills wholeness. Health is God's primary will for all his children, and disease is to be combatted in God's name and with his power and with every means available. The Kingdom of Health is within us, said Russell Dicks, and the keys to it are faith on the part of the patient and love and power on the part of the healer![1]

I firmly believe that all healing is divine. Every successful operation is the miracle of faith healing. Dr. Robert C. Peale, (a physician and a surgeon) brother of Dr. Norman Vincent Peale, writes:

> Because of the abiding faith and trust the injured or sick person has in Almighty God, as a surgeon, I constantly see recoveries that were thought impossible. I also see poor results because of an attempted cure by religion or science alone. I am therefore convinced that there is a definite and fixed relation between religion and science, and that God has given us both as weapons against disease and unhappiness, but administered together for the benefit of mankind, their possibilities are unlimited.[2]

That leads to two observations:
1. We ought to use every scientific means at our

disposal in healing. Christian faith and science are not enemies. The only time they are is when some scientist says there is nothing to religion or when some less-than-knowledgeable minister insists that science is atheistic. Generally speaking none of the accredited scientists today say there is no room for the spirit. In fact, some of the best advocates of faith in America are scientists like Wernher von Braun. These two areas complement each other, and are really part of one power: God.

Unfortunately, there are some medical doctors who see nothing but a mechanistic view of man and his body. Dr. A. B. Bond, a doctor in Philadelphia, once told of a professor he had in medical school. He opened his first lecture by saying, "Man has a body and a soul. That's enough for the soul. The next four years you will hear about the body." He dismissed the soul with one sentence, and Dr. Bond said the man was true to his promise. Nothing more was heard about the soul.[3]

Medical science, however, deals not just with the physical. The medicine of the person is the new medicine of today. I know a doctor who prays before every operation, "Direct me, O God, in performing this operation, for I am but an instrument in thy hands!" I know others who will kneel beside the patient's bed and pray if the occasion calls for it. Though science has swept forward with seven-league boots, it alone will not make us well.

2. We follow a false trail if we think there are no other powers in the universe for healing except those that yield to scientific reason. Man is a creature with more than physical needs. Our bodies are not just machines. When there is a car wreck and the police begin looking for causes, they not only examine the

machines themselves but they ask a lot of questions about the driver. He is as important as the machine, and in most cases more so! Our physical problems often root deep in emotional, spiritual, and mental needs.

Many doctors are deeply Christian and highly sensitive to this matter of spiritual healing. Once a doctor asked me to see one of his patients who was suffering from a severe heart condition. He was an anxious man, living in constant fear of the next heart seizure. I went to see him in the hospital and immediately felt the tension as I entered the room. The man had dug his fingernails into the flesh on his chest because of the severity of the pain. He blurted out, "Preacher, I don't know when the next one will come. Be prepared." I began to talk with him quietly about the power and love of God and repeated some Bible verses that I learned as a child: "The Lord is my shepherd. I shall not want" (Ps. 23:1). "They that wait upon the Lord shall renew their strength; they shall mount up with wings as eagles; they shall run, and not be weary; and they shall walk, and not faint" (Isa. 40:31). "Casting all your care upon him; for he careth for you" (I Pet. 5:7). Then I prayed for healing and wholeness. He relaxed, and before I left he was sleeping peacefully. Now he is a well man and is able to carry on his work in a sane and sensible way. He had been killing himself by his anxiety. You see, faith is not an escape, nor is it weakness. It is a weapon, often the only weapon for those who want to be strong and whole.

How does the Christian faith work in healing? What good is prayer for the sick?

For one thing, prayer and the Christian faith help by creating the proper emotional and spiritual attitudes for healing to take place. The Christian faith imparts a will to live, a will to be well, a positive attitude. No power on earth can overcome the lack of a will to live and be well! Prayer does not change the mind of God. His mind does not need changing. He is already on the side of health. But prayer changes our attitudes and our emotions by putting us in tune with what God wants for us all the time. When we, by prayer and faith, bring ourselves into harmony with God, we have a better chance of getting well and maintaining health.

A second thing about faith and prayer in healing is there are some functional diseases that no medicine can cure. Illness often comes when the destructive emotions get out of control. Several years ago I knew a man who was very sick, and although the doctor had examined him carefully, he couldn't find anything wrong organically. But one morning he died. When I asked the doctor what had killed him, he replied, "Hate." Then he went on to explain that years before this man had had a misunderstanding with another man whom he never forgave. He talked about his hurt constantly and died of hate. The doctor made this significant statement, "My medicine couldn't help him one bit!"

In America, the great problem of health is the destructive emotions. And it is here that the Christian faith can heal where medicine can't. There is no hope for many a sufferer apart from a spiritual rebirth.

A third thing about faith and prayer in healing is that it often takes place at once. Dr. Alexis Carrell, a reputed physician and scientist, wrote that he had seen a skin cancer disappear at the command of faith.[4] That was not breaking the laws of nature. It was rather the imposition of a higher law of life over a lower law, the fulfillment of the laws of nature or God's healing power. More than one doctor has told me that he has seen pneumonia destroyed in fifteen minutes and a patient's temperature drop from over one hundred degrees to normal. But today we have become so sophisticated and cynical that we don't believe such things are possible. Our emphasis is on obeying the physical laws. And I agree with that. God does nothing but by law. He has provided enough power within his laws, many of which we know nothing about, to do everything in accordance with his will. His will includes unlimited things that may look like miracles to us but which are actually the operation of his healing force. It is for us to learn his will, surrender to it, and seek the power and wholeness and health he has for everyone of us.

But what if physical healing is not possible? I go back to my topic: "Incurable is man's term—not God's." A disease may be incurable in terms of this physical life and must await a final cure in the next life. Dr. Carroll Wise has said:

> A person of real faith does not demand cure as the price of his faith. He can accept less, if this is what the realities of the case demand, and like Paul, find strength in his faith to live with a thorn in the flesh. Or if death is to be the outcome, he can accept this with serenity and peace. The man of mature faith is able to accept either life or death because he has lost his fear of both.[5]

One of the damning indictments of some faith healers is that the burden of proof is on the patient.

If he is healed, the patient is praised for his faith. If he isn't, it is implied that he has no faith. This is unfair. There are times when physical healing must be reserved for the next life, but even so there is a higher healing—that of spirit.

Someone has wisely said that in the final accounting the greatest discovery of all will be that of a divine reality that will enable us to stand anything that can happen to us. Dr. Weatherhead tells of a young woman who was taken to Lourdes, the famous shrine in France. She was given a silver cross which the priest had blessed. Too sick to take part in the processions, she was told to hold the cross tightly and pray that she would recover. She did as she was told, but to no avail. She went home to die. Dr. Weatherhead said that as she was dying, she gave the cross to him, and said, "I want you to keep it, for it has taught me a great lesson. I have learned not to hold the cross and try to believe that I shall be healed, but to yield myself to the crucified and not mind whether I am healed or not."[6]

What shall I do then about my illness?

1. Call the doctor. Have one you trust, one who believes in prayer, and that all healing is divine. Pray for him, pray for yourself, help him help you. He can't do it alone, but God can through him.

2. Call your pastor. I like to visit members of my church before they go to the hospital to help prepare them spiritually for the experience. Of course, I go to visit while they are there, and I try to use all the spiritual resources available for healing.

What a blessing it would be if pastor and people worked together in this matter. Jesus called twelve men together. They were as different as day and night, but he drew them into a unity of love that actually became an extension of his incarnation and power. The spirit of God worked through them as individuals and through the group to heal. And today the intercession of people united in love for Christ, living a disciplined life of prayer and Bible study, love and compassion can bring healing to people that may be impossible for medical science. How wonderful it would be if every church could have small groups to serve in this way: visiting the sick, praying for them, and assisting the pastors in the ministry of healing.

3. Put yourself in God's hands. This is God's life in us. The Bible points this up clearly, ". . . and breathed into his nostrils the breath of life; and man became a living soul" (Gen. 2:7). This life we enjoy is the gift of God. It works better when we acknowledge this fact and are committed to him and his way.

4. I must say something about healing that comes through one who acts as a receiver and a transmitter for God's power. We talk of praying for others, and we pray in a general sort of way, never believing that anything will happen. I believe that God gives those who are surrendered to him in love and faith the power to heal the sick! In other words I believe God uses people in healing. This is the instinctive method of love. Recall the times when you have gone to visit the sick. Remember the pat on the shoulder, the hand laid on the fevered brow, or the tightly clasped hands. This is a simple symbol of what I mean. Combine this human touch with the power of prayer, the strength of faith, and often there occurs what we call a miracle. God heals by the addition of a higher spiritual energy to a lower physical energy. Every person ought to be such a channel of God's power.

Incurable—Man's Term, Not God's

This is the most direct method of healing—praying for one another, the healthy for the sick, the loving for those who need love, the saved for the lost, the whole for the broken, the strong for the weak.

3

You Need Not Stay the Way You Are!

HUMAN NATURE IS NOT FIXED! We ask, "Can a leopard change its spots?" and we answer emphatically and with a note of finality, "No!" But there is a difference between a leopard and a human soul! Celsus, the Greek critic, once said, "Everybody knows from long experience with actual life that once a man has gone a certain length in sin and folly, there is no smallest prospect of reclaiming him, because inevitably the man is carried downhill faster and faster by his own impetus." This I refuse to believe!

Human nature is potential, and not fixed. We may become what we will. In his book *Human Nature and Its Remaking*, Dr. E. S. Hocking says that the gray matter in the brain is the easiest stuff in the world to change. Indeed, he says, every sense impression from outside keeps changing it every second. Dr. Hocking sums it up by saying, "To anyone who asserts as a dogma, 'Human nature never changes,' it is fair to reply, 'It is human nature to change itself!'"[1]

Because I like flowers and gardens so much, one of my heroes is Luther Burbank. He said once, "If I have made any worthy contribution to the world, it is that a plant born a weed does not have to remain a weed, or that a plant degenerated by conditions of nature, does not have to remain degenerated." Peas

You Need Not Stay the Way You Are!

and carrots are nothing but weeds that have been cultivated.

But over and over comes the refrain whenever some improvement is proposed, "You can't change human nature!" However, psychologists tell us that human nature can be formed, deformed, and reformed. It is the most plastic part of us, the most susceptible to change. Some of the laws of the physical universe are unchangeable. We can't change gravity, the rise and fall of the tides, the roll of the seasons, the rotation of the earth, the distance of other planets. These are fixed laws. But not so with human nature. The sins, prejudices, and failures that characterize our lives can all be changed, reversed, completely made over. John Dewey, one of the world's noted philosophers, said, "If human nature is unchangeable, then there is no such thing as education, and all our efforts to educate are doomed to failure." Psychology is based on the fact that ways of feeling, thinking and acting can be altered!

This is the heart of the Christian faith. Jesus set forth this mighty truth when he said to Nicodemus, "You must be born again"—a surprising statement to this learned leader of the Jews. What did it mean?

The word *conversion* means to turn around, to turn back, to change the direction one is traveling. The life that faced one way now faces another as a result of a conscious choice. And Jesus told Nicodemus that was what he needed to do: turn around. He had been born of a woman; that was obvious. Now he needed to be born of the spirit—to submit himself to God so that his life might be made over along spiritual lines. William James defined conversion as, "The process, gradual or sudden, by which a self, hitherto divided and consciously wrong and unhappy, becomes unified and consciously right and happy in consequence of its firmer hold on religious realities."[2] Jesus told Nicodemus he needed to have this happen to him, and this is what needs to happen to every man. And it can happen to every man.

Take Paul. He was born a Pharisee and grew up very zealous for his faith. Read Philippians 3:1-7 for a vivid description. According to his own words, he must have been a very divided, unhappy man, even though he was zealous in his religion. And incidentally, many an unhappy man or woman who is active in the church needs the experience of surrender to Christ that brings conversion. There was a time when Paul felt himself powerless to do right. "O wretched man that I am!" he cried. He was under the law, but the law had no final power to save, only to guide, or at times defeat. He was at war with himself, as well as against Christians. But on the road to Damascus he had an experience. He was blinded momentarily, and the return of his sight is symbolic of what happens in conversion. He saw life in a different way. What he once hated he now loved, and what he loved once, he now hated. Life for him was lived from a new center: "Nevertheless I live; yet not I, but Christ liveth in me" (Gal. 2:20). He came to order his life by the words, "I can do all things through Christ who strengthens me!" He said, "If any one is in Christ, he is a new creation" (2 Cor. 5:17). Paul meant here that when a human life is committed to Christ a revolution takes place and a new creation is brought into being. John Wesley put it this way: "Only the power that can make a world can make a Christian."

You Need Not Stay the Way You Are!

Here is a vital point: human personality can be changed at any age. No matter how old you are, you can start over, be converted, be changed in nature. Some of the happiest experiences of my life have been in connection with older people who had lived everything but the good life but who were changed and became good and useful persons.

Once I went to the hospital, at the suggestion of her doctor, to see a woman in her early seventies. He had made every test conceivable and there was no sign of an organic disorder. After talking with her for some time I became convinced that something out of her past was bothering her. She finally broke down and told me this story.

Years ago, she had been in love with a young man who assured her that they would get married. They had sexual relations, but he later informed her that he wasn't interested in marriage. She was brokenhearted, and as the years passed, she was guilt ridden. Ultimately she met and married a very fine man and had several children, but she always carried the fear that someone might find out about her past. She was sick from an overdose of guilt.

I asked her if she wanted to be well. She said she did, and I believed her. Then I told her of the little verse in the New Testament, "If we confess our sins, he is faithful and just to forgive us our sins, and to cleanse us from all unrighteousness" (1 John 1:9). I talked about how Jesus forgave those who crucified him and about how the past can be forgiven and forgotten. I asked her to venture out on what faith she had. She prayed, and then I laid my hand on her head, as I sometimes do, and said softly, "Your sins are forgiven!" I could see victory written all over her face. When the doctor came in, she told him she didn't need to stay in the hospital any longer, and he dismissed her. She was well. She had carried a sense of guilt with her for years that wasn't necessary. People can be changed, no matter what the age, or the need.

This experience of change may take place suddenly or gradually. Some try to fix a pattern and say it must take place in a particular way, but not even Jesus did that. He said that the Spirit of God defies all patterns. Jesus used the wind as an illustration . . . it blows where it will, and you can't tell where it came from or where it goes, ". . . so is every one that is born of the Spirit" (John 3:8). The wind comes, who knows how, cleansing, invigorating, freshening, and then it is gone. So does God break in, who knows when, who knows where, who knows how? It may be suddenly as we think of our lives and what we have made of them and see the desperate need. Or it may come gradually, like the opening of the flower to the sun as we see the contrast between what we are and what we can be. But back of all this is the undeniable fact: men and women can be transformed by the Spirit of God! First Corinthians 6:9–11 gives one of the New Testament's most magnificent pictures: "Fornicators . . . adulterers . . . thieves . . . covetous . . . drunkards . . . revilers . . . extortioners . . . such were some of you: but ye are washed, but ye are sanctified, but ye are justified in the name of the Lord Jesus, and by the Spirit of our God!" How magnificent! Nearly every man comes to the place where he says, "This is what I have made of life. It cannot be changed now." Everything in the Christian faith, everything in psy-

You Need Not Stay the Way You Are! 33

chology, everything in common sense says no! Human nature can be changed!

This is something that man does not effect alone, nor does God force him. I like to think of salvation as a partnership. It is God's gift. We must take it. That implies God's power and man's faith. We do not achieve it. We receive it. God is always ready to give. Someone has rightly said that God has already done his part. He has made his gift of forgiveness and reconciliation available in Jesus Christ, and now it remains for man to do his part: by faith receive it! John says, "As many as received him, to them gave he power to become the sons of God" (John 1:12). What we cannot do for ourselves alone, God does for and with us as we have faith and receive the gift. There are two parts to this: man's desire to be different, his deliberate willingness to turn from one way of life to another. Then God does his work of forgiving, renewing, restoring. The old life is exchanged for the new one! Henry Ward Beecher cried out in his search for a new life: "Lord, save me; here is myself to save me with; O use me for my own salvation!"

Conversion is but the beginning. It is not enough to put off the old life, surrender to God, turn away from old sins, and just have an experience called conversion. I have known people who were converted in one meeting after another, sometimes every summer in the annual revival meeting. It is most important to realize that conversion is just the beginning. Then there must follow a lifetime of spiritual training, education, discipline, service, and witness. Paul uses a phrase that I like, "To us who are being saved . . ." (1 Cor. 1:18, RSV). The Christian life is a continuous process. It begins. It grows.

The family and neighbors and our fellow workers can tell that something is happening to us, not just because we tell of an experience we may have had at a certain time and place, but because they can see a difference in our lives! Here is a boy who is careless with his speech, almost never combs his hair, uses a washcloth as little as possible, and can never find the Right Guard! But suddenly one day, his hair is combed, his shoes are shined, he's had a bath, and he's found the Right Guard. What happened? A pretty little girl moved in next door. You don't have to have someone tell you, you can see for yourself what a difference love makes in a boy! So with the Christian life. It is a different life, one of joy, one of good habits, one of love, one of clean speech, one of helpfulness, one of compassion for family and friends, one of new attitudes! When one falls in love with Jesus something happens! The Christian life is a growing life.

The transformations recorded in the New Testament are being repeated every day. Several years ago I performed a wedding. The couple was happy to the nth degree. It seemed that nothing could spoil their happiness, but something did. They began quarreling over little things—money, each other's relatives, the children that had now come along. Then one day she came to me and said that her husband had a new girl friend and was stepping out on her! Next he came and said his wife had a boy friend. They were both members of the church, but I suspected that they never had let the Christian faith take hold of their lives. I spent hours with them and discovered that neither of them was really a Christian. They were ashamed of the sorry mess they had gotten into and genuinely wished to make a new beginning. I felt that to talk about marriage problems was a waste of time. There was something else more important. So I talked with them about how people really start over, how the power of God can remake lives. I prayed for them, then each prayed for himself, and then for each other. They made a surrender to God. Today there is a new light in their lives. They have been converted. They started over again as persons, and because they did, they have been able to work out their troubles in marriage!

On occasion I pass through a part of our city that is everything but pretty. It is the place where they dump scrap iron, old bottles, rags, wrecked cars, broken machinery. Recently while going by I saw them loading great quantities of scrap iron onto a railroad car. It will go to a factory to be melted down and made into something new. Perhaps it will come out as surgeon's tools, fenders for another car, or needles. Who knows what. But it will be new. If man can do that with his old scrap iron, why not believe that God can do it with human beings too? He can, and he will. Your part is to trust him enough to yield your life to him. His part is to forgive, cleanse, make you a new creation. He'll do it right now. At least he'll make a beginning for you if you will!

4

Healing and Forgiveness

ONE DAY JESUS stopped by the pool of Bethesda. There were all kinds of sick, infirm, and aged people lying around it. A legend was popular that at certain times of the year an angel went into the pool and troubled the waters. Whoever got into the pool first after the troubling of the water was healed. There was one man who had been lying by the pool for thirty-eight years. He was brought there every day in the hope that this would be his day. Jesus saw him and knew that he had been there a long time. He said to him, "Do you want to be made whole?" That sounds like an odd question. Surely Jesus knew that a man sick for so long would want to be healed.

This man by the pool of Bethesda had it good. While everyone else was out working, he could lie in the shade, collect some handouts, receive the sympathy of people passing by, and be waited on hand and foot. Did he really want healing? He decided that he did, so Jesus said, "Get up, take up your bed and walk!" (John 5:1–16).

Can a sense of guilt growing out of wrongdoing have such an effect on a person physically, mentally, and emotionally that he cannot do his work or find peace of mind? Can one gain an assurance of God's forgiveness so that the sense of guilt will be lifted, resulting in healing of body, mind, spirit? The answer to both questions is yes!

Of course, not all illness is due to sin or a guilty conscience. However, much illness comes because man is out of harmony with his Maker. An unrelieved sense of guilt is one of the major causes of psychosomatic illness—that is, illnesses caused by the emotions. Such guilt can and does bring on all sorts of physical illnesses. Many a person has died from a sense of guilt. Dr. Alphonse Maeder, a famous European psychotherapist, has said, "On the basis of my experience as a psychotherapist, I can state that a large percentage of nervous diseases are illnesses of the conscience."[1] And so are a lot of the diseases of the body as well. An awakened conscience, ignored, will take revenge on mind, body, spirit. In short, guilt can make us sick.

Forgiveness and healing are closely linked. There are many people who will never know wholeness until first there is forgiveness for wrongs in their lives. A bad conscience can make a living hell out of life. Man is a unit. Spirit, mind, and body cannot be separated but must be treated as a unity. Man is not just physically sick, or emotionally sick, or mentally sick. He must be treated as a unit. In Jesus' work, often the healing of the soul and of the body took place simultaneously. He said, "Your sins be forgiven." Alienation from God, a sense of guilt, had to be cured before healing of the body could take place. Guilt feelings so beat a person down that he feels unworthy and may actually become sick. Many of our guilt feelings grow out of little things. But they can keep God out. And man's major need is to have God in!

In T. S. Eliot's play *The Cocktail Party,* Celia Copplestone confesses to her psychiatrist: "It's not the feeling of anything I've ever done which I might get away from, or of anything in me I could get rid of—but of emptiness, of failure toward someone, or something, outside of myself; and I feel I must atone —is that the word?"[2]

This play illustrates vividly the destructive power of a guilty conscience. The woman in the play was simply putting into words what is in fact an inner experience. Guilt feelings can play havoc, hinder, torment, cripple personality. Guilt can produce organic illness. It has driven people to suicide. It has created a feeling of need for self-punishment. We may escape detection in our wrongs by other people, but there is in every man a court of justice that not only finds him guilty, but also metes out punishment. The Bible is as new as this morning at this point: "Whatever a man sows, that he will also reap" (Gal. 6:7, RSV). "Be sure your sin will find you out" (Num. 32:23).

On another occasion some men brought a sick man to Jesus. The crowd was so great that they couldn't get in the door. So they tore off a part of the roof and let him down right in front of Jesus. Seeing their faith and the man's need, Jesus said, "Man, your sins are forgiven" (Luke 5:18–26). Jesus gave attention to the deepest need of the man—deliverance from a guilty conscience. These men wanted physical healing for their friend. Jesus knew a higher healing was necessary before physical healing could take place. After he had taken care of that, the physical ailment was easy: "Rise up and walk."

Healing and Forgiveness

We may say there is no God, nothing to religion, no absolutes in morals, but a person cannot explain away the misery that comes from knowing that he has wronged himself, or another, or breached the moral law. Nature simply won't take it.

The great need of human beings is harmony, inner calm, spiritual peace. And the chief mission of the church is to bring that healing and peace to people. John Henry Jowett, once pastor of Fifth Avenue Presbyterian Church in New York, said, "Out of the church must go forth vigorous healthy men and women who went in maimed and paralyzed. Broken things that no one could mend have been made whole again." E. Stanley Jones tells in *How to Be a Transformed Person* of a young man in Japan in one of his meetings. He leaned back over the bench and asked Dr. Jones, "Are you sure I am forgiven?" Dr. Jones assured him on the authority of Christ that he was. A few minutes later the young man leaned back and asked again, "Are you sure I am forgiven?" He assured him again. A third time, the young man asked the question and received the same assurance. Dr. Jones comments, "There is nothing, absolutely nothing that a man wants to know as much as to know whether his sins are forgiven."[3]

Forgiveness is fact. In the Old Testament, Isaiah wrote, "Though your sins be as scarlet, they shall be as white as snow; though they be red like crimson, they shall be as wool" (Isa. 1:18). All the prophets proclaimed this forgiving love of God, but it remained for Jesus on the cross to show the depth, the length, and the height of the love of God. Here is a love so mighty that it can absorb the worst that man can do and go on loving. Jesus said by his death that this is how much God loves you and wants to forgive you and make you whole!

John Bunyan wrote in *Pilgrim's Progress*, "So I saw in my dream that just as Christian came up with the cross, his burden loosed from off his shoulder, and fell from his back, and began to tumble and so continued to do, till it came to the mouth of the sepulcher, where it fell in, and I saw it no more. Then was Christian glad, and said, 'He has given me life by his death!' "[4] So he has. John writing long after the death of Jesus said, "If we confess our sins, he is faithful and just to forgive us our sins, and to cleanse us from all unrighteousness" (1 John 1:9). And Paul wrote, "For by grace are ye saved, through faith; and that not of yourselves: it is the gift of God: Not of works, lest any man should boast" (Eph. 2:8–9). The Bible speaks plainly of the desire of God to forgive men and make them whole.

How do you get that forgiveness? Faith is a criterion for wholeness. Jesus asked the man at the pool, "Do you want to be healed?" The man must have said yes even though the Bible doesn't say so. I am sure this man could see no way of healing, but he wanted it above all else. Faith is the deliberate choice of belief as against unbelief. We get rid of our guilt by humble confession to God, acceptance of the offered forgiveness of God, and a resolution to live the good life in his power. Faith is to believe that when we do these things, God does his work, keeps his promises. I feel my need, I make the first move by faith, then God does his work.

Perhaps this has been put too simply. Yet I am convinced that what I have said is the beginning of

Healing and Forgiveness

health for many people. There are millions of people who will never know physical health until first there is a confession of some wrong that keeps tearing them apart with a guilt feeling.

An attractive young woman was brought into the emergency room at a hospital. She had been stabbed in a drunken brawl and was so badly hurt that the doctors could see no hope. They did all they could, then assigned a young nurse to sit with her until the end came. As the nurse sat looking at the girl and thinking what a shame it was that such a pretty girl should go like this, the young woman opened her eyes.

"I want you to tell me something and tell me straight," she said to the nurse. "Do you think God cares for the likes of me? Do you think he could ever forgive anyone as bad as me?"

The young nurse was taken by surprise, for she had never before made her Christian witness to anyone else. She reached out her hand for God's help, and reached out in love to the young girl, until she felt a oneness with both. Then she said, "I'm telling you straight. God cares about you and he forgives you now."

The girl sighed and slipped back into unconsciousness. But as death came, the lines of her face relaxed into a smile. Something tremendous happened between God and that girl, and it happened through the nurse, who literally became the healer.

5

Learning to Face Up to Life

A COLLEGE PRESIDENT once remarked that after years of association with college students, he was uncertain whether the B.A. degree stood for Bachelor of Arts or Builder of Alibis! All of us resort to excuses and alibis at one time or another. This is a universal weakness.

Jesus was at dinner one day, and in the course of the meal he told what would probably be his funniest story if it didn't contain so much truth.

> There was a man who was giving a great feast, to which he invited many people. At the time for the feast he sent his servant to tell his guests, 'Come, everything is ready!' But they all began, one after another, to make excuses. The first one told the servant, 'I bought a field, and have to go and look at it; please accept my apologies.' Another one said, 'I bought five pairs of oxen and am on my way to try them out; please accept my apologies.' Another one said, 'I have just gotten married, and for this reason I cannot come.' (Luke 14:16–20, TEV)

Look at the humor. "A certain man made a great supper," is the way the story begins (KJV). Now, in Palestine there are no long twilight hours. When darkness comes, it is dark. It is dark at supper time. That makes these excuses show up for what they

Learning to Face Up to Life

really are. The first man had bought a field and just had to go look at it. In the dark? The second had bought some oxen and he just had to go and try them out. In the dark? But the third excuse is the silliest of them all. He had gotten married. Maybe she wouldn't let him go. But when you remember the place of women in the ancient east, this excuse becomes laughable indeed. Women were treated like inferiors, even though the plight of womanhood among the Jews was far above that of other ancient peoples. To hear a Jew refuse a free meal just because he had gotten married was ridiculous. The excuses are silly beyond measure.

But don't they sound familiar? Haven't we all made excuses for not doing what we knew we ought to do? This is a tragedy of excuses. We do not give excuses for the good and high choices we make but for the low and mean ones. And ultimately those who live by excuses lose the ability to discriminate between good and bad, high and low, right and wrong.

Much of the tension and unrest and nervousness in our lives comes because we do not face up to life and act responsibly. A psychiatrist told me that the happy people are those who accept responsibility for themselves and act accordingly. Much of our unhappiness comes because of our rationalizations and excuses. We can't bear to be put in wrong light. We simply do not wish to show up badly in the line-up of life.

All of us use excuses to avoid self-blame. If we do something wrong, it is a mistake; if others do the same thing, it is a sin. If we lose our temper, it is righteous indignation; if others do the same, they have no self-control. If some shoddy practice in business brings us gain, it is a stroke of luck; in others it is unethical business behavior. If we get involved with another woman, it is a harmless flirtation; in others it is gross adultery. And so we hide our desires, deeds, feelings behind excuses and refuse to take responsibility for ourselves. No wonder we have ulcers and are tense. Happiness comes to those who honestly face up to life, take responsibility for themselves, and act accordingly.

Someone has suggested four ways by which we try to evade responsibility: shifting the blame, romancing, pretense, and self-pity.

Shifting the blame. If you have children at home, you know all about this one. "He told me to," or "I couldn't help it," or "Johnny started it." We cast around for someone else on whom to blame our failures and wrong choices.

The story of Adam and Eve is a perfect illustration. God told them very pointedly not to eat of the tree of knowledge. But they did. They tried to hide from God, but when he found them, they began to rationalize. Adam looked around for an excuse. "It wasn't my fault," he said. "The woman gave it to me." I am sure he felt relieved. He had shifted the blame. In fact, God, you are to blame. If you hadn't made woman this would never have happened.

When the blame was shifted to her, Eve began to look around for an excuse. And she found it. There was a snake handy. It was all his fault. Actually, God, this is all your fault. If you hadn't made the snake, and if he hadn't egged this thing along, we wouldn't be in trouble.

God turned to the poor snake. The snake didn't

Learning to Face Up to Life

say a word. He took responsibility for his actions. You know, Adam and Eve left out the greatest *if* of all: "If we hadn't yielded to temptation!"

How familiar. If it hadn't been for the politicians, if it hadn't been for the Russians, if it hadn't been for the blacks, if it hadn't been for my grandparents . . . and we miss the greatest if—if we had done what we ought to have done, and if we had made the right choices!

A man came to see me about his marriage. It was falling apart. He listed all the things wrong with his wife and her family. He bitterly lambasted the neighbors for being so nosey. But he left out the most important if of all: "If I had done a little differently myself."

I talked with another man about his job. He was failing. He blamed the boss, his associates, fate. But it never dawned on him to take blame for his failure himself. We say, "If I had married someone else" or "If I had another job"—but honestly now, if these conditions prevailed, would we be any better, or happier? So often we think if we correct outward circumstances we will find happiness. But our lack of happiness and peace is mostly within ourselves. We have to find peace and poise within, or we won't find it. A poet has said:

> We sing the song of a tropic isle,
> That lies in a turquoise sea,
> Of happiness and a peaceful home
> In the shade of a breadfruit tree.
>
> The weather is perfect all the time
> And the air is virgin pure,

> A tropical isle is the place to live
> To be healthy and secure.[1]

But many a person who has found his outward circumstances to be near perfect has not found peace. "It's not what you'd do with a million, if fortune should ever be your lot. But what you're doing at present with the buck and a half you've got!" Shifting the blame is popular sport.

Romancing is a way of fictionalizing out of something we do not want to do. Two men were out on the lake fishing one Sunday morning, and the church bells began to ring. One said penitently, "You know, Sam, we really ought to be in church this morning!" Sam thoughtfully rebaited his hook and answered, "I couldn't go anyway. My wife is sick!"

"What can I do? I am so little and the problems are so big!" "I won't be missed among so many!" The romancer is always making big plans but never carries them out. He sighs for the good old days and dreams of the time when men were men. A man told me that he wished he had been alive in Jesus' day. But I knew his record. He was just romancing and was doing nothing about being really alive in his own time.

Pretense is an ugly word, but it is also a way of excusing ourselves. We hide behind smoke screens. There is the reason we give; then there is *the* reason. For example, look at the reasons why people don't go to church. "I got enough religion when I was a boy. My parents made me go!" "This is my only day to rest. I work six days you know." "There are too many hypocrites in the church." A woman actually told me that she didn't attend church because she could not

Learning to Face Up to Life   47

do without a cigarette that long. One particular man told me that his dog broke his leg and that visiting hours at the animal hospital were from eleven to twelve o'clock on Sundays and that he'd just have to go. These are some of the reasons given, but the real reason is that we are more interested in something else.

Take our pretenses for wrong doing. There is the reason we give. Then there is the *real* reason. "If I only worked somewhere else . . . you can't work where I do and be a Christian." "You just can't be honest in business these days and make a living!" (This one stands up just long enough to find one honest businessman.) "Everyone else is cutting corners . . . everybody's doing it!" These are the excuses given. The actual reason is there are no inner braces to hold us up, no master, no central loyalty.

There are pretenses for not taking a moral stand in the face of wrong and injustice. "It is none of my affair." "None of my family drinks." "My children don't do those things." "My vote doesn't count anyway." "There aren't any blacks in our area." "I don't want to get involved." These are the reasons given. The real reason we don't stand up when faced with moral wrongs and injustices is that we are cowards.

Self-pity is another way by which we evade responsibility. Poor health, no money, wrong side of the tracks, no real opportunity—how familiar! Did you ever stop to realize that much of the world's progress has come through men and women who have had handicaps: Paul had a thorn "in his flesh," John Milton was blind, Robert Louis Stevenson had tuberculosis, Beethoven was deaf, Jesus was born on the wrong side of the tracks in a stable, George Washington Carver was black, Fanny Crosby was blind. These men and women didn't have much of a chance either, and each of them could have excused himself because of poor health, wrong side of the tracks, inadequate educational opportunities, or a dozen other things. The reason we give is one thing. The real reason is something else again. Self-pity is never an adequate excuse for refusing to take responsibility for ourselves and our behavior.

Consider what happens to us when we excuse ourselves in these ways. Living by excuses robs us of joy. Look again at the story in Luke 14:24, ". . . none . . . shall taste." This means that none of those whom he had invited would enjoy the dinner. I wish I could have been around that day. I suspect the three men who were invited, but who excused themselves, went by the king's house later on in the evening to see how things were going. Imagine their surprise when they heard laughter and sounds of joy coming from the palace. They were doubtless crestfallen because they were missing the fun that might have been theirs. This is the tragedy of hiding behind excuses, pretense, self-pity, romancing: we lose the real joys of life. The things we thought we wanted seem so trivial later on. The very excuses we use bring disgust when they have run their course. We allow our passions to run riot, we live by rule of thumb, we get ours while the getting is good, we have a good time with ourselves; but in the darkness of the bedroom, with none to see but us and God, there is an emptiness that just won't let us be happy. We need something to fill the void. Excuses rob us of joy.

But to excuse ourselves is to rob life of any possibility of growth and development. On the other

Learning to Face Up to Life

hand, to take responsibility for ourselves and face up to life is to grow in character and spirit. The excuses given by the three men in Jesus' story sound logical. They are all right. It is important to buy and sell land. It is good to own capable oxen. And every man needs a wife. But these things must not be first in life. Growth in character comes when we learn to put first things first and give second-rate things second-rate loyalty. Jesus laid down a basic principle for great living when he said, "Seek . . . first the kingdom of God, and his righteousness and all these things shall be added unto you" (Matt. 6:33).

To excuse ourselves is to show up the real weakness in our character. We use excuses to evade the ugly truth. We need to look good in our own eyes, and we do not want others to know the real truth about us. So we use excuses to hide cowardice, hatred, lust, greed—in short, we use excuses to mask the truth about what we are and what we want in life. Character dies, growth stops, and we lose the real joys of life when we live by evasion and excuse. *Only those people are happy who take responsibility for themselves.*

We are personally responsible for what happens to us. We may curse the fate that is ours, rationalize, blame heredity, circumstances, the government, and even God with our shortcomings and failures. But the final question in every person's life is going to be: "What did you do with your life?" In time every man will stand before God, stripped of all pretense, self-pity, rationalizations, romancings, and be judged on the basis of what he has done with what he had. And God will not consider excuses.

I am a very frank admirer of George Washington Carver. It is startling how his life's story in *Who's Who* begins and ends. It begins: "Born of slave parents who were killed by northern soldiers." It ends: "Fellow of the Royal Society, London." Few men contributed as much to the development of the South. The boll weevil struck in the early nineteen hundreds. Dr. Carver was one of the first to see the necessity of diversification of agriculture. So he studied the peanut and suggested in his own county in Alabama a shift from cotton to peanuts. They did so with amazing results. Later that county erected a monument to the boll weevil that reads, "In profound appreciation of the boll weevil and what it has done." Out of the fertile brain of Carver came countless ideas for the use of the peanut: coffee, bleach, axle grease, filler for wood, linoleum, shampoo, meal, soap, and many other useful products. Suppose he had said, "I'm just a Negro, of slave parentage. All I can do is hoe cotton and get by until I die!" He acted responsibly for himself. And so must every person if he is to grow, know joy, be useful, be well-pleasing to God.

So what do we do?

1. Frankly face up to limitations. All of us have them. We can use them. Military experts tell us that no war can be won by defensive action alone. There must be attack, aggression, thrust. Jesus might have avoided Jerusalem. But he set his face steadfastly to go to his Jerusalem. E. Stanley Jones defines offensive living: ". . . a frank facing of life—letting it speak its direst word—then taking hold and turning it to victory." If you have problems, face them. Bad temper, unruly sex urges, harbored grudges, handi-

Learning to Face Up to Life　　　　　51

caps, family problems, whatever they are, face them.

2. Have a dominant purpose. With a central purpose there is no need for excuses. Not just any purpose will do either. Hitler had a dominant purpose, and the world was bathed in blood because of it. John D. Rockefeller had a dominating purpose: make money. Khrushchev had a dominant purpose. But not just any dominating purpose will do. Jesus summed up the highest purpose in life when he said, "You shall love the Lord your God with all your heart, and with all your soul, and with all your strength, and with all your mind; and your neighbor as yourself" (Luke 10:27, RSV). This is responsible living. It combines love for God, self, and neighbor. It gives life breadth, height, and depth. God has made us free to choose the way we will go. The whole, healthy man deliberately chooses the long-range goals, the lasting values, the true purposes in life. The dominating purpose for him becomes to do the will of God. When a man has a central loyalty, a dominating purpose in life, excuses aren't necessary. Dr. Edgar S. Brightman wrote:

> Everybody wants something. The practical man is the man who knows how to get what he wants. The philosopher is the man who knows what he ought to want. The ideal man is the man who knows how to get what he ought to want.

The whole man is the man who knows what he ought to want and sets out to get that through the power that God affords.

3. There is *one* who can deliver us from evasion and excuse: Jesus Christ. A young man came to him

one day and asked about the good life. Jesus told him in simple terms, "You must be born again!" We must realize that we cannot make ourselves what we ought to be. The tendency to make excuses is engraved into human nature. Such a deeply ingrained attitude requires radical surgery to remove it. But to be a Christian doesn't mean putting on some new virtues, some new ideals, nor does it mean passing new resolutions. We must be made new inside out. The heart must be changed. Only Jesus Christ can make a new person. He can give a new center, a new heart, a dominating purpose. With a new heart, we face up to life, take responsibility for our sins, our abilities, and face the future with power and purpose. This is God's doing, not our own. It happens when we surrender ourselves to him.

In his book, *The Man Who Lived Twice*, Eric W. Barnes has given us the biography of playwright Edward Sheldon. Sheldon was made almost helpless and immobile by arthritis. Later, he became completely blind. But this man found a faith and was able to triumph over his affliction. While his distress was at its height, he wrote Van Wyck Brooks, "I never felt the need of a definite religion until recently. I used to think I could stand up to anything that came along, but I don't anymore." In the book is this paragraph:

> During the next weeks he came to grips with destiny and from some hidden reservoir of the spirit drew strength to go on. He not only found the courage to endure under a blight from which death might have seemed a welcome release, but he formed the sure belief that affliction could not destroy the purpose of his life . . . in the moment

Learning to Face Up to Life

of crisis he found a faith which would not only sustain him in the thirty remaining years of his life but which would reach out in powerful and mysterious ways into the lives of other people![2]

And the faith that lifted Edward Sheldon above his affliction is available to each of us. We don't have to live by excuses and rationalizations. We can face up to anything that life brings and overcome in the grace and power that Jesus gives.

6

Forget Yourself into Usefulness

ONE DAY A LEPER approached Jesus on the road, and I can imagine how he felt: "Nobody loves me. Everybody shuns me. I'm a leper. My family—nobody—will have anything to do with me. Why me? It shouldn't happen to a dog. If you want to, Jesus, you can help me." His leprosy was bad enough, but his self-pity was worse. Jesus took him by surprise. "Of course I want to. Be clean."

This is no dusty, out-of-date story. But it can be repeated over and over again. Do you remember the lines learned in childhood:

> Nobody loves me. Everybody hates me,
> I'm going out and eat some worms!

Our tendency when things go wrong is to feel sorry for ourselves. We become convinced that nobody cares—nobody suffers like we do. We're convinced that we are really great and don't deserve the hard times that plague us. We seem to delight in nursing our grievances and hurts, and frequently we manage to nurse them into major disasters. A noted psychiatrist once said that one-third of his patients suffered from the devastating malady of feeling sorry for themselves. This is just a symptom of something far

Forget Yourself into Usefulness 55

deeper—the sickness of self-centeredness. Someone described a very self-centered woman this way: "She was bounded on the east by Edith, on the west by Edith, on the south and north by Edith."

Three things happen to us because of self-pity. In the first place, it kills the possibility of making the most of our lives, our potential. F. Scott Fitzgerald died at the age of forty-four just when he ought to have been coming into his own. He died of self-pity. His first novel *This Side of Paradise* was a success. His second, *The Beautiful and the Damned,* was a miserable flop. Now that's a pretty good batting average— one out of two. Most people would settle for one out of ten and feel good about it. Writing books is treacherous business. Once you put your ideas on paper, they can haunt you forever. The critics were hard on Fitzgerald. He felt put-upon. One of his biographers said he "surrendered to failure." He began to drink; he mistreated his family until his wife broke down physically and mentally. Fitzgerald's genius was destroyed by self-pity.

Several years ago, Dr. Pierce Harris, then pastor of First Methodist Church, Atlanta, had an article in the church bulletin entitled "How to Be Perfectly Miserable."

1. Think about yourself.
2. Talk about yourself.
3. Use *I* as often as possible.
4. Mirror yourself continually in the opinion of others.
5. Listen greedily to what people say about you.
6. Expect to be appreciated.
7. Be suspicious.
8. Be jealous and envious.
9. Be sensitive to slights.

10. Never forgive a criticism.
11. Trust nobody but yourself.
12. Insist on consideration and respect.
13. Demand agreement with your own views on everything.
14. Sulk if people are not grateful to you for favors shown them.
15. Never forget a service you may have rendered.
16. Be on the lookout for a good time for yourself.
17. Shirk your duties if you can.
18. Do as little as possible for others.
19. Love yourself supremely.
20. Be selfish.

Self-pity and self-centeredness destroy any possibility of our making the most of our lives.

In the second place, self-pity keeps us from living happily with other people. It makes us resentful, irritable, and often cruel. Seneca said, "In thoughts of self-commiseration a man will discover no advantage but will rather incline toward deterioration and softening of himself and with these will come upon him a growing indifference to his fellowman." After all, a man engrossed in his own miseries has no time for the miseries of others. To be self-centered is life's greatest insanity. It makes love and health impossible.

In the third place, self-centeredness destroys man's right relationship with God. When the self-centered man tries to pray or read the Bible or worship, it turns to a self-pity session. Our prayers can become a sad enumeration of our troubles. We complain of what God is doing or not doing. Self-pity is an out and out denial of God and his mercy. A. E. Housman gives poignant expression to this feeling of self-pity:

Forget Yourself into Usefulness

> And how am I to face the odds
> Of man's bedevilment and God's?
> I, a stranger and afraid
> In a world I never made.[1]

Self-pity means we judge God by our troubles rather than measuring our troubles by God's grace and mercy. We talk too much about our problems and not enough about God's power.

Somerset Maugham's novel *Of Human Bondage* was really a reflection of his experiences as a boy. The boy in the story was clubfooted and ashamed of his deformity. He would pray at night to be well, then in the morning he would feel down under the covers to see if he had been healed. The clubfoot was still there, and the boy was angry and disappointed. Maugham had grown up with a stammer as a result of his rejection as a child. He would curse God. In the story he had the boy reflect what he himself felt, "God is a lie! All the promises of hope and life are lies." Maugham forgot all the hurt, humiliated people who did not pity themselves but took their failures as challenges and built great characters. These, through faith in a God, won victory.

George Matheson was a brilliant young man engaged to a lovely woman. When he discovered that he was going blind, his bride-to-be rejected him. He struggled with himself and with God, both over his blindness and his rejection. Faith won. Out of his struggles a magnificent hymn was born:

> O love that wilt not let me go,
> I rest my weary soul in thee;

> I give thee back the life I owe,
> That in thine ocean depths its flow
> May richer, fuller be.

You see, self-pity can cut us off from the very source of our power and strength—God.

How can we handle self-pity successfully? Faith in Jesus Christ is the beginning of the answer in every case. No man can save himself. If we could, out of pure selfishness we'd do it just so we could brag about it. New Year's resolutions won't help. Most of our resolutions are broken before dark of the day we make them. We can't lift ourselves by our own bootstraps. Our emotions are stronger than we are. We try a lot of things: self-help books, psychiatrists, mental hospitals. Sometimes these help us by getting us to relax so we can think straight, but the real help lies in another direction.

Dr. Carl G. Jung, the father of modern analytical psychology, said that we need the ministry of a high religion in the gift of "faith, hope, love." When Jesus saw the leper, he said. "I will. Be clean." He did for the leper what the leper never could do. This was his way of saying, "God wills your health of body and mind and spirit." We begin to be healed when we surrender to this magnificent Jesus, who is God in flesh, and begin to follow him as the ideal of our lives.

It was Job's meeting with God that set him free from self-pity. He had suffered: lost his wife, children, cattle, health. But then he begged to see God face to face that he might plead his case and defend himself. But when he came face to face with God, he saw only God's greatness and goodness. He lost his sense

Forget Yourself into Usefulness

of self-pity. "I had heard of thee by the hearing of the ear, but now my eye sees thee; therefore I despise myself, and repent in dust and ashes" (Job 42:5–6, RSV).

The first step in overcoming self-pity is to take your eyes off of self and turn them to Jesus. When you really see him and put yourself by faith in his hands, you forget self. There are many ways to confront God: great music, silent stars, time of illness, the kindness of a friend, the beauty of nature. But I believe it is in moments of worship and prayer that we confront him best. As we read about Jesus, his life, his teachings, his death, his ever-living spirit, we see God—his greatness, his beauty, and somehow our little selves don't matter so much. It is wonderful what Jesus Christ can do with a human being.

A second step in handling self-pity is to form a picture of what you really want to be. Many of us never become anything different or better because we do not set a goal in life. We are content to drift, to live from hand to mouth, day to day, with never a dream to stretch the imagination. You become what you think about. Think positively, creatively, and you become something worthwhile. Think negatively, self-pityingly, and you become cynical and narrow.

Another step in handling self-pity is to get involved in the lives of others. This is exactly what a self-centered person cannot do. It can happen when a person gets his eyes off of self and on God. Then by forming a mental picture of what he wants to become, he begins to see his fellows in a new light and get concerned about them. Here is where a lot of our social activism falls apart. For many of us it is just busyness with no real foundation. We seem to be building an ever-increasing structure of social action on an ever-decreasing foundation of faith in Christ. That won't stand up. But when we begin to look away from self to God, we see people in a new perspective and get interested in them for new reasons. Our desire to help is no longer a selfish one but a consuming desire that everyone have all that God wills for them.

A newspaper reporter in Tucson, Arizona, once asked Dr. Karl Menninger, "Suppose you suspect that you're heading for a nervous breakdown. What should you do?" You'd think this great psychiatrist would suggest that you see a psychiatrist. But this is what he said, "Go straight to your front door, turn the knob, cross the tracks, and find somebody who needs you." A doctor told a man in New York who had suffered from pains in his neck and shoulders for years to go down to Grand Central Station, find somebody in trouble, and help him. You can't pity yourself when you are busily engaged in helping people because you love Christ and want people to love him too.

Dr. William S. Stidger tells of a minister friend in Chicago who had a peculiar way of curing his weariness. He would go to a businessman friend and ask for fifty dollars and then go on a unusual expedition. He would gather up the hungriest, poorest, neediest looking children he could find on the streets of the slum section and take them to a movie and then to dinner. After one of these trips, when the children had finished eating, a little boy came and stood in front of the preacher. When asked if he had had enough to eat, the boy replied, "I can still chew, but I can't swallow." Later another little boy came and just stood in front of the preacher, looking at him

Forget Yourself into Usefulness

with awe. The preacher said, "Do you want something more, sonny?" The boy shook his head, no. "Do you want to talk with me?" The little boy nodded no. "What do you want?" the man asked. "I just want to ask you something," the child replied. "All right, go ahead and ask me, sonny." The little boy looked him straight in the face and asked, "Be you God, mister?"[2] This little boy had learned somewhere that God is generous, kindly, loving; and the acts of the preacher seemed to that hungry child almost Godlike in his meager world. What a way to cure self-pity and weariness!

Forget yourself into usefulness! Take your eyes off self and, as the old hymn says, "Turn your eyes upon Jesus. Look full into his wonderful face and the things of earth will grow strangely dim in the light of his glory and grace."* Then form a clear mental picture of what you want to become. Get involved in the lives of other people. You'll be well on the road to being well!

---

* Copyright 1922. Renewal 1950 by H. H. Lennel. Assigned to Singspiration, Inc. All rights reserved. Used by permission.

7

Learn to Accept What You Cannot Change

WORRY IS COMMON to all people, at one time or another. Dr. C. F. Bradley has said that some children are born worried. He has found that cases of skin allergy and dental decay, attributable to nervous tension on the part of the mother, are found increasingly among newborn babies and children under five years. It is Dr. Bradley who said there are so many sets of twins born because babies are afraid to be born into a world like ours one at a time![1] Henry Ward Beecher said, "It is not work that kills men, it is worry. Work is healthy, you can hardly put more upon a man than he can bear. Worry is rust upon the blade. It is not the revolution that destroys the machinery, but the friction."

There is a fine prayer that goes like this, "God grant me the serenity to accept the things I cannot change; the courage to change the things I can; and the wisdom to know the difference." The novelist, E. M. Forster, wrote, "One has two duties: to be worried and not to worry!"[2] What a strange paradox. This is the gospel of learning to live concerned and unconcerned at the same time. Let's explore these two ideas that seem to be so contradictory.

In the first place, life is obviously a battlefield. Dr. Paul Tillich put it well in his book *The Courage to*

Learn to Accept What You Cannot Change 63

Be when he said that life is an arena between Being and Nonbeing, between forces that make for good, creative life and forces that restrict and destroy. How can any one live without tension in the face of the conflicts and the sense of meaninglessness that plagues us all today?

Then, too, there is a widely prevalent feeling of boredom, for which so many people take drugs and pills. And there is an ignorance of what really matters in life, the inability to distinguish between true and false values. Jesus asked the question, "Why labor for the food that perishes? Labor for the food that endures to eternal life." To add further to the milieu of confusion, there is the question of death—never knowing when or where. Plans for a great future or a brilliant career can be interrupted so suddenly. James says in his letter, "Just a moment, now, you who say, 'We are going to such-and-such a city today or tomorrow. We shall stay there a year doing business and make a profit.' How do you know what will happen even tomorrow? What, after all, is your life? It is like a puff of smoke visible for a little while and then dissolving into thin air. Your remarks should be prefaced with, 'If it is the Lord's will, we shall still be alive and shall do so-and-so'" (James 4:13–15, Phillips).

There are the things—pain, physical handicaps, sorrow—that come to us for which there seem to be no reasons. The reasons given for suffering make little sense or give little comfort: ignorance, our interdependence, our willfulness, the natural laws of God. For instance, a widowed mother stands by helplessly and sees her only son throw his life away in senseless living. A husband whose wife has such a mother fixation that their marriage is threatened. In another family, the husband and father is stricken with an incurable illness. No wonder Albert Camus called this the century of fear.

We have a cat named Tarbaby who is nearly fourteen years old. He is part of our family. The truth is, he dominates our family. During a recent Christmas, there were a lot of people coming and going. One night I saw Tarbaby hiding under a bed, only his eyes showing, peering out at passing feet. I have often felt like doing the same thing—hiding out somewhere but able to watch what is going on.

One of the world's largest and most luxurious steamships advertised, "You are miles away from worry on the world's fastest ship." But getting away from worry is not a matter of speed, distance, or luxury. Some of you will remember "The Eddie Duchin Story." Eddie was a cocky young pianist, succeeding beyond even his wildest dreams. He had life by the tail. But then it began. He suffered one tragedy after another. He lost his beautiful wife, and while he was still young, he discovered that he had a lingering disease for which there was no cure and which gradually robbed him of the ability to make music. At first he was rebellious, "Why do they have to destroy a guy. Just when it gets good, they take it away. Why?" He had been unable to believe that anything could keep him from getting his way. Now in the closing years of a young but successful life he tried to teach his young son what had been so hard for him to learn. He explained that he must go away. The little boy burst out with the old Duchin spirit, "No one can tell you what to do!" "Yes, someone can tell us all what to do!" There is enough in this world to worry us all into a mental hospital. And it does so increasingly.

Now let us examine the second idea. Look at the paradox with which we began: concerned–unconcerned. A paradox is something that is seemingly absurd but actually true, something ridiculous but verified in experience. That is what we confront here. Let's look at the life of Jesus. He was concerned and unconcerned. Jesus' life was outwardly one of the most troubled lives ever lived: tempest and tumult, tumult and tempest, the waves breaking over it all the time until the worn body was laid in the grave. But the inner life was a sea of glass. The great calm was always there. At any time you might have gone to him and found rest. "Come to me, all who labor and are heavy laden, and I will give you rest" (Matt. 11:28, RSV). Even when his enemies were dogging him in the streets of Jerusalem, he turned to his disciples and offered them as a last legacy, "My peace I give to you; not as the world gives . . . Let not your heart be troubled" (John 14:27, RSV).

Jesus' concern was for other people, and this is what makes him so different from us. He was human, and he must have given many thoughts to his own life and to his future as we do. But his major concern was not for self but for others. In a real sense he was a revolutionary, a freedom fighter.

The state of affairs in Palestine concerned him. He hated to see people treated like animals, to see them lost in the seeming meaninglessness of life. Anything that threatened to destroy human personality caused him deep concern. He grieved to see men sin away their possibilities and dash their dreams by foolish choices and deliberate wrong living. One day he went into the temple, took up a little whip, and drove out the money changers—those that bought and sold —because they were cheating the poor and making a profit in the name of religion from those who had no profit to give. Jesus was concerned, but his concern was for others.

The picture Jesus gave of the last judgment is a powerful one, "I was hungry and you fed me, thirsty and you gave me drink; I was a stranger and you received me in your homes, naked and you clothed me; I was sick and you took care of me, in prison and you visited me" (Matt. 25:35–36, TEV) —or, "I was hungry but you would not feed me, thirsty but you would not give me drink; I was a stranger but you would not welcome me in your homes, naked but you would not clothe me; I was sick and in prison but you would not take care of me" (Matt. 25:42–43, TEV). The test is to know there is sin and hurt in the world and not really see it, or feel it, or try to do anything about it.

Unfortunately, we are all wrapped up in our own aches and pains, ambitions and desires. Our concern is over whether people will like us, whether our clothes are better than someone else's, whether we are being cheated or not, whether we are getting what is coming to us. Our concern is for ourselves almost exclusively! So much of our anxiety is useless, wasted! Jesus said, "Do not be anxious" (Matt. 6:34, RSV). He did not mean that we should not make plans for the future. It surely wasn't his intention that we be Pollyannish in our attitude toward life or refuse to face up to the facts of suffering, sorrow, death, or the problems that every human being faces. He knew

Learn to Accept What You Cannot Change 67

that we must be concerned and anxious—that we would worry.

Well then, what did he mean, "Do not be anxious"? He meant simply, do the best you can and leave the rest to God! Jesus did this. He did the best he could for himself and for the people with whom he worked and then he committed it all to God. He said, and I suspect more than once, "Father, into thy hands I commit my spirit!" Or, "Nevertheless, not as I will but as you will!" We are to do the very best we can in a given situation and then leave the outcome to God without becoming fretters about it. Jesus believed something very deep: he believed that everything is in the hands of God. Do you?

Now, there is no question but that our anxieties are real. Peril and crisis are upon us all the time. But suppose we had to face the problems and perils of tomorrow absolutely in our own strength! What would we do? I honestly believe a person can suffer loss of job, loss of loved family members, or illness if he is convinced that God, not these things, has the last word.

Art Linkletter asked a little boy, "Son, what would our world be like without God?" The little boy replied, "We'd be in a mess." Anne Douglas Sedgewick, an English novelist, was very sick in her seventies. She could not breathe unless she was lying down; she couldn't eat unless she was sitting up. She said, "Life is a queer struggle. Yet life is mine and beautiful to me. There is joy in knowing I lie in the hand of God."[3] Here was the secret of Jesus' concern and unconcern. He did the very best he could, and then knowing that he and all life were in the hands of

God, he didn't worry about it! Such a conviction gives us a sense of personal significance and worth. To know that God knows us, cares for us, and is concerned over what happens to us ought to be the most exciting news on earth. This is the starting place for everything else. Personal salvation that leads to involvement with other people brings inner peace.

To come to the point where we can be concerned and unconcerned means that we have to spend time in God's presence. The French gave us a fine phrase, "Time to belong to oneself!" This means time away from the hurry and rush when we get things in proper perspective. How desperately we need that time away when we can look at ourselves as we are and talk with God about ourselves and then about the world. Find a quiet time somewhere for reflection, prayer, devotion.

Dr. Elton Trueblood writes: "A man has made a step toward genuine maturity when he realizes that, though he ought to perform kind and just acts, the greatest gift he can provide others consists in being a radiant and encouraging person. What we are is more significant, in the long run, than what we do. It is impossible for a man to give what he does not have."[4]

Our social consciousness ought to develop out of a "rich life of devotion." There can be no authentic outer life unless there is first an authentic inner life. The outward journey will lead to nowhere unless it begins in an inward journey of faith, prayer, reflection, and study.

Jesus wants us to be concerned about other people. It is one thing to fret away our lives over our own personal slights and insults, desires and ambitions. It is quite another to give ourselves in concern over the hurts and needs and sins and lostness of other people. Far too many of us concentrate on the assurance of personal salvation, yet are blind to human needs. The gospel does not find completeness alone in its personal aspects. Christianity is spiritual, but it is more than spiritual. We must not produce inner feelings that do not lead to outer involvement. John Donne said in his *Devotions,* "I am involved in mankind."[5] The danger lies in being only self-centered and not also brother-centered. We must develop the fine art of caring about other people, of becoming involved in their needs and longings! This is really worrying the right way.

In it all, learn to trust God. Do your best and leave it all to him. The Golden Gate is the inlet from the Pacific Ocean to San Francisco Bay. In a storm this passage of water can become a terrible, dangerous thing. On the ebb tide, especially under a blanket of fog and darkness, small boats can be carried out to sea before they know what is happening. Thirty-five years ago, engineers built a bridge over the Golden Gate. They went deep into the solid rock at either end of the bridge and built towers to carry the span. Cables were strung between towers anchored in solid rock, and from cables they hung the bridge. That bridge was built with a margin of safety to carry all the traffic that could be sent over it. People walk unafraid across the Golden Gate and traffic moves over it through storm and stress because support is anchored in rock on either side. Those whose lives are anchored in God can do the same with life. Do the best you can and leave the outcome to God. He can be trusted. Learn to accept what you cannot change.

8

Change Your Attitudes and You Change Your Life

As A MAN THINKS in his heart, so is he." The word *heart* had a different meaning for the biblical writer of these words than it has for us. We are heart conscious, and usually mean the organ that pumps blood to all parts of the body. But you wouldn't say, "I love you with all my pump!" The ancients meant much more. It was for them the center of life, the entire man, life power. In this verse from Proverbs, the meaning is: whatever gets hold of you in your innermost being is the thing that controls your life. Whatever we really think about, dwell upon, give ourselves to, that is what controls our lives.

Life is determined by attitude. Dr. Viktor Frankl, the Austrian psychiatrist who was confined for so long to German concentration camps, describes his experience in a thought-provoking book *Man's Search for Meaning*. He has this marvelous paragraph: "We who lived in concentration camps can remember the men who walked through the huts comforting others, giving away their last piece of bread. They may have been few in number, but they offer sufficient proof that everything can be taken from a man but one thing: the last of the human freedoms—to choose one's attitude in any given set of circumstances, to choose one's own way."[1] The world around us seldom

Change Your Attitudes and Your Life

determines what we are. Circumstances do not make us. Our attitudes determine what kind of world we really live in. Ralph W. Emerson said, "A man is what he thinks about all day long." Captain Eddie Rickenbacker wrote, ". . . if you think about disaster you will get it. Brood about death and you will hasten your demise. Think positively and masterfully, with confidence and faith, and life becomes more secure, more fraught with action, richer in achievement and experience."

It is one of life's tragedies that people blunder through life when the whole thing could be different if they learned and practiced the simple principles of the Christian faith. But so many people are negative, pessimistic, seeing no hope for anything, nothing but disaster for themselves and their world.

A man went to Europe. When he came back, all he could talk about was the fact that his hotel window in London wouldn't open. He never saw the greatness of London, or Paris, or Rome. The vast Atlantic didn't impress him. A stuck window! Recently I talked with a man in a small town who had just made his first trip to Atlanta. He had seen a warning somewhere, "Beware of pickpockets." He didn't mention Stone Mountain, the Cyclorama, the zoo, the stadium, or the tall buildings, and he didn't say a word about the great churches or the civic center. All of the beauty and grandeur of the city was lost because he had become obsessed over watching for pickpockets.

Many of us whose addresses show that we live on the third or second or even the first floor of our houses or apartments actually live in the cellar all our lives in our attitudes. What I think determines what I am! A little girl said to her mother at bedtime, "Mother,

I've had such a happy time today." The mother wanted to know what made it different from other days. "Well," the wise little one answered, "yesterday, my thoughts pushed me around—today, I pushed them around."

Take the matter of success. One great tragedy is that many people fail in life who do not need to do so. Henry David Thoreau said, "Men were born to succeed, not to fail." William James insisted that "the individual lives far within his limits." Destiny is not a matter of chance. It is a matter of choice. Every man chooses his own destiny by his attitudes toward life. Today we put too much dependence on methods and not enough on attitudes. You may use the latest methods in selling, but if you don't bring right attitudes toward your product, yourself, your customer, you'll fail. A book salesman knocked at a door one day and to the lady of the house said, "Lady, you don't want to buy any books, do you?" No, she didn't. Success means being able to free our minds from whatever shackles us. Anything that inhibits the flow of spiritual power through us defeats us.

Let's look first at the problem of our habits. Is there a person who does not have a habit he would like to kick? Almost all of us have some habit that keeps us from becoming what we'd really like to become. It may be unseen by the world, and yet it gets a hold on us and threatens our security. It may be drinking, or smoking, or profanity, or gambling, or self-pity, or being too critical of people, or greed, or worry, or wrong thoughts. Habits of long standing do get a grip on us. A little boy was angry with his mother and was running away from home. A neighbor saw him standing on the corner and asked where he was going. He told the neighbor he was running away from home. "Well, why don't you go on?" "I'm not allowed to cross the street," replied the boy. Habits may throttle our initiative and stifle our best selves. But our attitude toward the habit is the determining thing. If we go on saying, "I can't break this. It has too much hold on me," we'll never stop. There is no habit that cannot be changed if we want to change it!

Then again, I think the attitude many have toward happiness bears looking at. It is amazing how many people think sad, negative thoughts all the time and never seem to feel happy or be happy. I preached several months ago on happiness, and a first-year student in one of the schools of theology really took me to task. He said he was in complete revolt against the happiness seekers. Happiness was not an adequate goal or purpose in life. He went on to say that no one knows what happiness is. He is right. I am in revolt against the happiness seekers if by that you mean the people who think happiness is getting, or going, or doing, or just having fun, no matter how. But the whole point in Christianity is that it intends for us to be happy. Jesus gave some important steps for finding it (Matt. 5). Happiness is a by-product of being something. It comes to the person living in right relationships first with God, with self, and then with other people. Jesus said, "These things I have spoken to you, that my joy may be in you, and that your joy may be full" (John 15:11, RSV). Joy releases people, sets free creative attitudes. The gloomy, grouchy man seldom really succeeds.

Attitudes of prejudice, particularly race prejudice, are literally destroying millions of people. They'll never know any happiness until they learn that all people are God's children, at least in potential, and that we can love people of all colors and stations in life. In the highest meaning of the word love, we will work for the very best in life for them just as we do for ourselves and our own. Someone has said, "Don't worry about what shows from without but the love that lives within." I must admit that I have been troubled in the past by race prejudice. I am sure I have wished that we could maintain the status quo and go on as we had in the past. But that has not been Christian. I have tried very hard to rid myself of this prejudice by working with people from a wide variety of racial backgrounds and really getting to know them.

A judge who lived in Fayetteville, North Carolina, was certain that nothing good could come out of the North. One day he stood admiring a beautiful magnolia tree in a nearby yard. A younger man came up and the judge said to him, "John, that is the prettiest tree in the world." "Yes, judge, it is a pretty tree," replied the younger man. "John, do you know what makes that tree so pretty?" John spoke of the green leaves, large flowers, and so on. "No," the judge interrupted, "what makes the magnolia so beautiful is that it won't grow above the Mason-Dixon Line."

Our attitude toward the church is also very important. If we think failure, the church will fail. Never in history has so much been said about the faults of the church, her irrelevance, her littleness, her slowness. I admit the failures of the church, and I could name some that her worst critics haven't thought of yet, but there is still more good in the church than bad. The way to change things in the

Change Your Attitudes and Your Life

church is to change our attitudes toward the church and begin to build instead of destroy. Nothing is ever built by destructive criticism. It is interesting to me that some of the people most critical of the church are the first to call on it in times of desperation and need. And the church always responds, gladly. That is what the church is for. It is not perfect. The church is not a club for saints, but it is a school for sinners—of which I am chief! I owe the church a debt I can never pay. So does all mankind. From a negative pessimistic attitude toward the church—your church—turn to a positive, constructive one.

The New Testament is very plain about this matter of attitude. If you want a changed life you must change your attitude. Paul put it bluntly, "If any man be in Christ, he is a new creature: old things are passed away; behold, all things are become new" (2 Cor. 5:17). This transformation is within. Jesus said it to Nicodemus: "You must be born again." That is, change the whole direction of your life. We begin to live when Christ begins to live in us. Our lives are not just improved or altered a little bit. This is more than some new resolutions, an outside paint job. A change is made that is so radical that a man can be called a new creature. The old has passed and the new has come. This may well refer to attitudes. When a man is in Christ, as Paul so often said, his old attitudes of prejudice, negativism, hatred, failure, unhappiness are done away with and new attitudes come to take their place: attitudes of love, hope, optimism, purity, giving. The difference is an inner change in which our attitudes are no longer ingrown, but focused on Christ. The new man lives in a new world, works at a new place, lives in a new house—not that any of these have changed, but the man has changed. This is what John Masefield was saying in "The Everlasting Mercy" as he described the change that came over Saul Kane, the poacher, the drunk. "O glory of the lighted mind, how dead I'd been, how blind! The station brook to my new eyes was babbling out of Paradise . . ."[2] This was the same old world, but how different it looked to a man who had finally submitted his life to Jesus Christ. You don't have to remain the way you are. Change your attitude and you change your life, and your attitudes are changed when you yield up life to Jesus Christ and begin to follow him in earnest.

Years ago the Barber's Supply Association held a convention. As a publicity stunt, they went into the skidrow section of the city and found the worst drunk, the most unpromising man they could find. He was unshaven, emaciated, sad. He was taken to a hotel, given a bath, a shave, a haircut, a new suit, overcoat, shoes, and even spats. When they finished, he was a marvelous example of the barber's art. The story appeared in the daily papers. The manager of the hotel was impressed. He told the man he would give him a job and back him and make a successful man of him. He was told to report for work at eight o'clock the next day. Eight o'clock came, but the man didn't. He didn't show up all day, so the hotel manager went to look for him. He went back where they had found him in the first place. There he was, sleeping on some newspapers in an alley, drunk, new clothes gone, barefooted, unshaven. The moral to that story ought to be plain: it is never enough to clean a man up on the outside. You'll never make anything of

Change Your Attitudes and Your Life 77

him until there is a change in the inside—in his attitudes! The same truth applies to poverty and cleaning up the slums. It is not enough to give a man money or a new house. He needs a new heart, a new attitude first. If we don't learn this and begin our rehabilitation program with changed attitudes, then new housing projects become slums and welfare grants perpetuate misery.

Somewhere I read the story of a little boy who was born with a withered leg. He had to wear a leg brace all his life and never could run like other boys or climb trees. He reasoned it out himself. If he could not compete with others in play, how would he ever be able to compete with them in business in the world? So the fear began to grow. But his father was a wise man. He said to him, "Son, don't worry about the leg. Someday I am going to take you to the cathedral and there before the great altar, God will heal you."

The day came. Father and son, dressed in their very best, went into the church. They walked down the aisle hand in hand, little boy hobbling along on his crippled leg. They knelt and the father said to the boy, "Son, pray and ask God to heal you." They prayed. Later the boy described his father's face when they finally lifted their heads after earnest prayer. "Never before had I seen such unearthly beauty as was upon his countenance in that moment." The father put his hand on the boy's shoulder and said with feeling, "Son, let us give thanks to God. You are healed." The boy was impressed. Standing up, he looked down at his leg and saw that it was the same. A flood of disappointment engulfed him. They started walking out of the church, but as they got almost to the great doors, suddenly the boy stopped. "All of a sudden, I felt something tremendously warm in my heart. Then I seemed to feel something like a great hand pass across my head and touch me. It was as light as eiderdown, but I can feel it to this day, the delicacy and yet the strength of the touch. All of a sudden I was wondrously happy and I cried out, 'Father, you are right. I have been healed.'" Boy that he was, he knew that God had not taken the brace off his leg, but he had done something much more important—he had taken the brace off his mind. It would be a wonderful thing for God to heal a withered leg, and I am sure he could do it. But it is a greater miracle to heal a wounded mind, to strike off the braces that shackle, and give a man changed attitudes—make him a new man. When that happens, he can bear anything, endure anything, accomplish anything. To change your life, change your attitudes!

9

The Dull Monotony of Over and Over and How It Is Healed

THE GOOD LORD never meant for any life to be bored! A famous doctor once said: "After all, the most deadly of human diseases is one which we cannot touch with a knife or save people from with drugs." "You mean cancer?" he was asked. "Oh, no. We'll get that little devil, or devils, yet. I mean boredom. There is more wretchedness, more torment driving people to folly, to what you parsons call sin, due to boredom, than to anything else!"

I was talking with a young housewife who had gotten into the habit of drinking heavily. She said, "The only explanation I can give is that I am bored stiff with just staying at home, looking at four walls, washing dishes, cooking meals, and changing diapers!"

A classic example of boredom is that of Betsey Patterson. She was reputed to be America's most beautiful woman. In 1804, Napoleon's brother, on a visit to America, became infatuated with her and they were married. Napoleon had the marriage annulled. Toward the end of her life, Betsey Patterson said:

> Once I had everything but money. Now I have nothing but money. I am dying with boredom. I am tired of reading, and of all the ways of killing time. I doze away my existence. I am too old to flirt, and without this

stimulus I die of boredom. The princess tries to keep
me up to the toil of dressing by telling me I am a beauty.
I am tired of life and tired of having lived![1]

Boredom is not an immediately destructive emotion. However it leads directly to, and is responsible for, more illness, disruption of lives, and crime than any of us ever dream. We seem ready to do almost anything to break away from boredom, except the one thing that will handle it.

Many marriage problems grow out of the fact that two people have gotten in a rut. The glamor of courtship wears off, and the routine of married life settles in. Here is a chief cause of infidelity in marriage. Monotony takes over and marriage partners seek excitement elsewhere because they are bored. I was talking with a man one time about his relationship with his wife, and he said, "What's the use of chasing the bus after you've already caught it." His marriage was about to break up over dull boredom and routine.

I am convinced that many young people become juvenile delinquents because of boredom. Someone said, "Many a young person goes to the devil because there's no place else to go." I heard of a boy who broke a thousand windowpanes in a factory. Why? Was he a bad boy? No. He was looking for something to do to fill an empty place in his life. Bored. Here is one reason why the church must be in the business of recreation for young and old. Recreation is important, for it helps in part to fill a gap in life.

How many days do you get up wishing you had one of those glamorous jobs in Hollywood or New York instead of the dull, boring one you have? As modern

The Dull Monotony of Over and Over

life becomes more and more mechanized, monotony will become an even greater problem unless we discover the origin of it and get at causes instead of symptoms. Years ago, the government set up weather stations in out-of-the-way places over the world. One was at Severdrup Island. They asked for men to man them. Each application was studied carefully, and every man was asked why he would be willing to go to such a lonely place. One young man, a sales clerk, said, "The trouble with my setup is there isn't enough 'me' in it. I eat breakfast at the drug store and let the bus driver take me to work. At night I sit back and hope the television comedians will make me laugh, or I pay to be amused at the movies. I can look back on almost any day without finding one where I felt important." A secretary pounds the same fifty keys on the typewriter every day . . . a workman punches the time clock at 6:58 every morning . . . a housewife washes the same dishes day after day . . . a truck driver rolls over the same miles. Life gets so daily.

Even wars are brought on by boredom. Clifton Fadiman said, "The Crusades were stimulated in part by love of God, in part by love of loot, and in part by the terrible tedium of daily life." Men follow a Hitler because he promises escape from boredom. Some Englishmen deplored the end of World War II because they felt there was nothing more to work for to unify them.

This sense of futility, melancholy, and world weariness which has settled on the human spirit is only another proof that modern man, for all his brilliance in some dimensions, has missed the main thing. He has tried to live as if he were a child of this world only;

he has given his attention to things, set his affection on the world only, and has forgotten his kinship with the infinite—the one dimension that gives his life significance.

We must go deeper. The whole problem is emptiness. T. S. Eliot sums it up for the poets when he uses such phrases as "Leaning together, headpieces filled with straw . . ." Someone else said: "Fed up at fifteen, fagged out at forty!" There are six million alcoholics in the United States, sick people, primarily because their lives are empty. We take tranquilizers. Three hundred million prescriptions were filled for them last year. We take narcotics, smoke marijuana, take LSD, and do a thousand other things to fill up the empty space inside us. As someone has said, "When we are not filled with the Spirit, we have to turn to spirits!"

There are all kinds of drugs besides those I have named. Action becomes a drug when we run dizzily from thing to thing to keep from feeling empty inside. Amusement becomes a drug when we sample all sorts of things trying to find an antidote for boredom. When night comes to any modern city, masses of people swarm into night clubs and places of amusement looking for an hour's diversion to forget the emptiness of home or the futility of work. It is not too much to pay a comedian ten thousand dollars for one evening's performance to provide such diversion for empty people. Don't misunderstand me; diversion is essential. The reason for seeking it is what matters. If it is our crutch, the only thing that keeps us from putting a gun to our temple, then it is wrong. If it is to add spice to an otherwise full life, then it is good.

One afternoon, I was sitting in our living room. Bill

The Dull Monotony of Over and Over

was playing his trumpet, and Elizabeth was accompanying him on the piano. Lassie, our old dog, was lying with her paws over her ears. Charles had a little car operated by two batteries and he had set the wheels so that the car went in circles, round and round. As I watched the car, I saw that I, too, go round and round. So do you!

We are made for greater things than we are getting. So much attention has been given to outer space that we have neglected inner space. We spend our time and energy in a search for something to cure boredom, for something that will put a solid foundation under life, for something that will stand in the changes of our day. And hope that if once we can find that something life will click for us and we'll never be bored again. But, in my opinion, the only antidote for the devastating feelings of boredom is for our lives to be firmly linked with the eternal. A moment's pleasure is not enough.

One of the greatest scenes in the New Testament is Jesus' encounter with the woman at the well in Samaria. She had had five husbands, and the man she was living with at the time was not her husband. She came to draw water from the well, and Jesus asked her for a drink. Being a hated foreigner and a woman, she was astonished. They got to talking. Then Jesus spoke one of his most amazing words: "Whoever drinks this water will get thirsty again; but whoever drinks the water that I will give him will never be thirsty again. For the water that I will give him will become in him a spring which will provide him with living water, and give him eternal life" (John 4:13–14, TEV). Another time he said to his disciples, "The thief comes only in order to steal, kill, and destroy. I have come in order that they might have life, life in all its fulness" (John 10:10, TEV). The implication here is that God offers a style of life that is full and complete and lasting—a quality of life that leaves no room for boredom.

I firmly believe that faith in Jesus Christ and complete surrender to him can take the boredom out of life and make it full and exciting without all the external crutches we use. You'll note my use of the word *surrender*. A noted psychiatrist recently defined surrender as "a moment when the unconscious forces of defiance and grandiosity actually cease effectively to function. When that happens the individual is wide open to reality. He can listen and learn without fighting back. He is receptive to life and not antagonistic. He senses a feeling of relatedness and at oneness which becomes the source of an inner peace and serenity."[2] He was talking primarily about alcoholism and the way out of it. But surrender is the way out of boredom too. Jesus said to those who heard him, "Follow me." He might have added, "And I will show you the way out of boredom, defeat, uselessness, sin, and whatever else it is that spoils life for you." And when we by faith accept him as Lord of our lives, to follow him up to the limit of our ability, then life begins to be exciting and full. Thomas Chalmers entitled one of his sermons "The Expulsive Power of a New Affection." Jesus said, "You must be born again!" Both mean the same thing. There must be a new center for life, a new master, a new sovereign. And when Jesus is that, we just can't be bored!

A dozen or so years ago, the Auca Indians in Ecuador murdered five missionaries who had come to help them. The whole world was shocked by the stories.

Nate Saint and his four companions had prepared the way as best they could for the first contact with them by dropping pictures and food before the missionaries landed. But shortly after they landed they were attacked and murdered.

But the effort was not lost. Kimo and Komi, two members of the Auca tribe, later gave this witness. Kimo said, "We used to be very bad. We lived in darkness because we didn't know Christ. Now we have Bible." They had been taught to read the Bible through the efforts of Rachael Saint, who went to them after her brother had been killed. She taught them not only to read, but she led them step by step to a commitment to Jesus Christ. One of them said, "We have had our hearts as well as our bodies baptized." A few years ago, murderers; now a part of God's redemptive purpose in the world. If such a transformation can take place in Ecuador, it can take place in Panama or Atlanta or wherever you are. The great antidote for boredom, for a misspent life, for hatred, is a faith in Jesus Christ that transforms deeply, completely!

It is in Christ that we discover the meaning of life. Even the most tedious job can become rewarding when we see that job in the light of its contribution to the welfare of man and how it fits into God's scheme of things. Our work becomes satisfying when we are Christ's, and we work, not just to get money, but to help people.

Marriage takes on new light and life when we have Christ in our hearts. I have found few problems in counseling that would not yield to faith in Christ.

When we are his we begin to live outside of self and for others. Life isn't boring when we are genuinely interested in other people and their needs and wants. It is self-centeredness that makes life boring! I occasionally get a letter from someone in the United States government. In the upper right hand corner of each envelope is the legend, "Penalty for Private Use." Well, there's a penalty for private use of our lives too. That penalty is boredom. But when we set our affection on things above, and our hearts are centered on Christ, selfishness goes, and our concern is for people. You can't be bored when that is true.

> Several years ago, a group was planning to honor Albert Schweitzer. He was brought to America. The University of Chicago planned to give him an honorary degree as a part of the celebration. Dr. McGifford went with a group to meet Dr. Schweitzer at the train. They saw him get off the train. They greeted him and told of their joy in having him. Then he disappeared. They couldn't find him. He had slipped away. When they did find him he was carrying a suitcase for an old woman. They looked around at each other and wondered why a man as great as Dr. Schweitzer would do a thing like that. It was so much a part of his life, his Christ-inspired life, that it was just the natural thing for him to help somebody. Then Dr. McGifford said, "I wish I could find an old woman whose suitcase I could carry!"[3]

Life is boring for a lot of us. Here is an answer! "Keep your minds fixed on things there, not on things here on earth." That's it. Give your heart, your affections to Jesus. Say to him by faith, "I accept you as the Lord of my life; I accept your way as the way of life. I will follow you up to the limit of my ability!" Something will happen. You'll be a new person. There'll be a new center for your life. You'll never be bored again!

10

The Healing Power of Hope

THE MOST PROFANE WORD in the English language is not one of the four-letter words so widely used. It is rather the word *hopeless*. The most sacred is hope!

In twenty-five years in the ministry, I have never sensed the feeling of hopelessness that seems to be abroad today. It is actually a matter of crisis. To be without hope makes us physically sick. It leads to things that destroy both mind and body. Frequently in counseling, I hear, "I just don't see any way." A young editor who seemed to have everything, but whose life apparently was empty, wrote: "I'm up against a blank wall. Evenings I get drunk, or rub the snout of my gregariousness against the fur of other animals in an almost frantic effort to get relief from myself. The great majority of days are so filled with banality that all talk of purpose, meaning, and high morality seems a strange sort of cant."[1] How do you get out of this rat race? The world situation, disturbances on college campuses and in the streets, a war in Vietnam, racial wars all over the world, the economic plight of millions of people, vast ignorance over the world, disregard for human dignity—it is easy to get a sense of hopelessness and despair.

A young man climbed high on a bridge, preparing to jump. A policeman came along and caught him by the coattails and dragged him down. "What do you mean trying to take your own life? It can't be that bad. Think of all the good things in the world." The boy listened stolidly. The policeman continued, "Tell you what. You list all the bad things, all your problems and troubles. Then I'll tell you all the good things in the world and all the reasons for living. If you still want to jump, then I won't stop you." So the boy listed his problems, the troubles in the world. Then he and the policeman locked arms and both jumped into the river!

To most of us there come times when darkness seems to close down around us, and the morning seems so far away. Emptiness, lack of love, the loss of spiritual and moral standards, the impersonality of the age take away hope and fill us with despair. Marcus Aurelius put it pointedly when he said, "Up and down, to and fro, round and round: this is the monotonous and meaningless rhythm of the universe. A man of ordinary mental powers who has reached the age of forty has experienced everything that has been, is, and is to come!" Then why live?

How many things there are in the world to discourage us. But more importantly, how many things there are inside us to plague us, to threaten us, and finally to destroy us unless we can lay hold on hope. We take pills, and there are times when pills are essential to give relief and bring rest and relaxation. And if one brings some relief, think what forty might do! The pain would be gone forever. No more dark nights of wrestling, turning, doubting, hurting! But what of the hurt such action would bring another for years, another who loves us, and who might never be able to understand?

The Healing Power of Hope

Each year twenty thousand people take their lives, and every four minutes someone tries. Suicide is not limited to the old and infirm but is increasing among teenagers and college students. A college vice-president said recently that his school had had the largest number of attempted suicides in history. What brings an intelligent person to the place where he sees no solution to the riddle of life except to take the final route of escape? Many reasons are given: sickness, economic problems, family problems, revenge, pressures. Psychologists report that one of the major reasons is that while we have plenty to live on, far too many of us have nothing to live for, no sense of purpose, no far-reaching hope, that makes life infinitely worthwhile. But this is also true for millions of people who will never make any attempt to take their lives. They just go on breathing, eating, sleeping, running through the days, with nothing to challenge them to great living. Futility and hopelessness paralyze the souls of more people than we know.

Several years ago I was talking to a group of down-and-outs at Union Mission in Atlanta and used Kipling's "If" to try to stir their imagination.

> If you can force your heart and nerve and sinew
> To serve your turn long after they are gone,
> And so hold on when there is nothing in you
> Except the will which says to them: "Hold on!"[2]

From the back of the room came a thin voice, "And, preacher, what if you can't?"

The man was clean cut, well dressed, good-looking with the build of an athlete. He seemed perfectly calm as he announced that he was going to take his life. We talked awhile about most everything—his problems, his family, his work. Finally, he said, "I wish someone could prove to me that life is worth living!" I talked about hope, about faith in Christ, and all the possibilities there seem to be in life for me. He just sat and stared. Then he thanked me for my time, and for what I had said, and got up to go. As he left, he said again, "I wish someone could prove to me that life is worth living." He walked out, got in his car, drove three blocks, pulled to the curb, and shot himself in the head!

There are degrees of depression and hopelessness. Suicide has been described as a "hostility which turns inward." Dr. Russell Dicks suggests several symptoms of depression: a feeling that life is not worthwhile; tearfulness, although not always; a heavy mood in which the sufferer is unable to laugh or respond to wit, although he may normally be a responsive and witty person himself; the rapid onset of the mood—that is, it comes on in a few days or a few weeks in contrast to a lifelong pattern of worry; usually, although not always, a loss of sexual interest; a feeling, and frequently the expressed belief, that the sufferer has committed the unpardonable sin, although he can seldom describe what it is; slowness of speech and comprehension; and almost always the desire for death.

To be able to live with hope is one of life's greatest blessings. I do not mean that we are to be unrealistic, that we are to look at life through rose-colored glasses. Hope doesn't mean that. Dr. Samuel Johnson once said that to have a bright outlook on life was worth a thousand pounds a year. Every doctor knows the importance of hope. The Medical

The Healing Power of Hope

School at Cornell University made a study of the effects of hope on the human body. Dr. Harold G. Wolff wrote an article for *Saturday Review* in which he said that when a man has hope, he is "capable of enduring incredible burdens and taking cruel punishment."

An interesting proof of this fact involved the twenty-five thousand American soldiers imprisoned by the Japanese during World War II. Some of these men lived terrible lives, suffered inhuman treatment, worked under unbelievable conditions, and many of them died. Some of the men who worked and lived under the same conditions did not die and did not seem to suffer much from their months in prison, poor food, and hard labor. These men did not necessarily have more physical stamina nor were they naturally better men than those who died. The one difference seemed to lie in their ability to hope, to live in anticipation of the day when they would be free and home again. They drew pictures of their future homes on the prison walls. They described the girls they would marry. They studied as best they could the things they would need in their work in the future such as math, economics, business management. Some of the doctors even organized medical societies. Hope kept many a man alive in prison camp.

I talked with a young man recently who was headed for Vietnam. He was positive, hopeful. "I'm going over there, do what I'm supposed to do, learn all I can, do whatever good I can, and come home and go into the business for which I am prepared!" Hope is the virtue that keeps men alive and growing and standing on tiptoe every day. No wonder Paul included it in his famous trilogy, faith, hope, and love. It is no frail, fanciful, wish-it-were-so sort of thing. Hope is made up of blood, guts, tears, a positive affirmation of life and the anticipation of a blessing to be received.

What is the source of hope? Dr. Harold Roupp, a great preacher, used to say, "The religious person is not long discouraged, for it is the nature of religion to inspire hope in its followers." The deep hope of the religious person lies in his convictions about God, the universe, man, and everlasting life. Dr. L. P. Jacks once wrote, "Christianity is the most encouraging, the most joyous, the least repressive, the least forbidding, of all the religions of the world."[3]

The New Testament is a book of hope, but that hope is not centered in man and what he can do. Without God, man is just a cultured, educated, and sometimes civilized animal. With God there is another ingredient, a power, though unseen, that draws man upward, outward, onward, keeps high his hope, transforms his fears into courage. Remove man's hope in God and you have defeated him. Couple his genius with hope in God and the whole world is his.

We can hope that we need not remain as we are. Recently as I was coming out of a barber shop, a man stopped me cold and said, "I don't want to stay like I am!" You don't have to. No man does. I have seen alcoholics transformed by reason of their faith in God. Dullards have taken on new life. Sex deviates have changed their ways. Dishonest, greedy, vulgar, hateful men have become new creatures through their faith in Christ. The plant specialist can take a rough briar out of the field and graft a lovely rose onto it. The briar becomes a new plant, with new flowers,

The Healing Power of Hope

infinitely superior to any it produced before. So a man with faith in God becomes something new and different and wonderful.

No matter how hard and trying the days may be, the Christian has hope to carry him through. Hope is the Christian's armor to keep him from being defeated. Blows may fall thick and fast; his head may be bowed and bloody. He may lose loved ones in death; life may do its utmost to destroy him. When we go to Washington, D.C., I always like to go to the Washington Monument and the Lincoln Memorial. These two men, immortalized in stone, lived through some of the hardest days in our history. What brought them through? Hope for a great country, a united country, a nation where each man is of infinite worth and dignity. Like Abraham of old, of each of these it could be said, "For Abraham, when hope was gone, hoped on!"

People with hope get things done. Edwin Markham once said, "All that we glory in was once a dream!" Watts, watching his little engine run, said, "You see it working for the first time with the physical eye. I saw it working a long time ago in my mind's eye." Walter Reed envisioned an end to yellow fever. Jonas Salk foresaw a future with no polio. Thomas Carlyle, writing about the black days of the French Revolution, said: "O blessed hope, thou sole good of man: whereby on his straight prison walls are painted beautiful and far reaching landscapes, and into the very night of death is shed holiest dawn. Thou art to all an indefeasible possession in this God's world."

Our hope for the future keeps us going. I am thinking not of the future of this life only but of life after death. As I have knelt by the bedside of dying people, my convictions about immortality have been strengthened. For the pagan, there was hope only for the young. His life stretched out before him. But the Christian has forever. He knows this life is not all, that life is of a piece. We are born, we live, we die, we go on living. I have always been fascinated by the Roman catacombs into which the early Christians escaped to worship in privacy and in which many of them died for their faith. Knowing they faced death themselves, they buried their loved ones with such inscriptions as "Victoria in Christ and in peace." They knew there was more to life than seventy short years. I make a lot of trips to cemeteries with families. I like to say to them, not to startle them, but to reassure them, "He is not here! He is with God! He is alive! He is not dead!" I feel sad for people who do not have this hope. Whittier wrote:

> Yet love will dream, and faith will trust,
> Since he who knows our need is just,
> That somehow, somewhere, meet we must.
> Alas for him who never sees,
> The stars shine through the cypress trees!
> Who, hopeless, lays his dead away,
> Nor looks to see the breaking day
> Across the mournful marbles play!
> Who has not learned in hours of faith,
> The truth to sense and flesh unknown,
> That Life is ever lord of Death,
> And Love can never lose its own![4]

In preparation for a series for a religious emphasis week on a college campus, I wrote adult leaders on several campuses for suggestions. I asked, "Do you think a sermon on life after death would be appropriate?" The adults were unanimous in saying no! Do you know what was the second question asked in the inevitable midnight bull session? "Tell me preacher, do we go on living, or . . . ?" His voice trailed off as if he hesitated even to speak the word! Hope for continuing life makes this one richer, fuller, gives us a sense of security, dignity, worth that nothing else can give. The early disciples could lay down their lives for justice and truth simply because they knew there was more beyond!

In "The Trial of Jesus" John Masefield pictures Pilate's wife talking with a Roman soldier who took part in the crucifixion. She asks what he thought of Jesus' claim. "Lady, if a man believes a thing enough to die for it, he will get plenty of others to believe also." The she asks, "Do you think he is dead?" The soldier replies, "No, I do not!" "Where then do you think he is now?" she asks. "Let loose in the world where neither Roman nor Jew can stop him!"[5] Such is the Christian hope, the hope that heals!

11

On Loving Yourself the Right Way

MANY OF OUR DEEP personal problems arise from a lack of proper self-love. Many of the sins of which we are guilty we just could not commit if we thought of ourselves in the right way. Some think that while it is virtuous to love other people it is sinful to love oneself. We have been guilty of thinking that we must mutilate, despise, degrade ourselves in order to be Christian. For example, we look at the verse of Scripture that says, "If any man would come after me, let him deny himself," and we think that means that we must deny ourselves every good thing. Actually, our Lord is asking us to give up only one thing —ourselves. We are to deny ourselves first place and give it to him. He is not asking that we degrade, or despise, or mutilate ourselves to prove our love for him. It is assumed that to the degree to which I love myself, I do not love God or others. We are guilty of thinking that selfishness and self-love are the same thing. They are not. Calvin in his *Institutes* calls self-love a pest. But selfishness in a person is most often caused by a lack of proper self-love. If it is a virtue to love my fellow-man as a human being, it must also be a virtue to love myself properly, for I too am a human being. There is no concept of mankind in which I am not included. To love one's

On Loving Yourself the Right Way

neighbor as oneself implies respect for one's integrity, uniqueness, and dignity. Love for, and understanding of, one's own self cannot be separated from respect, and love, and understanding for another individual. A proper attitude of love toward themselves will always be found in those capable of loving others.

Dr. John S. Bonnell tells of a woman who came at the close of a Sunday service and said to him, "Pray for me, for I am terribly lonely, and feel that I cannot pray to God for myself. I have no friends. Your sermon made me feel that there might be some help for my loneliness!" He asked her why she had no friends, and she said, "There was a time when I had friends, but I have lost them all. In the last four years they have all become estranged. I haven't a friend left in the world, I haven't even God anymore. I have said and written hateful, cutting things!" She admitted that she had been having difficulty with her landlord and every other person whom she met. Dr. Bonnell said to her: "Tell me now, why do you hate yourself so much?" She asked in surprise, "Who said I hated myself?" Dr. Bonnell answered, "I know that you do. Your bitterness to others is hatred of yourself that you have projected on to others and to God!" Then she said, "I do hate myself, but I never realized that I had projected it on to my friends and that this is the explanation of my bitterness to others!" She went on to explain that years before she'd had an affair with a married man. She felt guilty and just couldn't forgive herself. Then the minister told her of God's love, and they knelt in prayer. When she got up, she said, "I feel as though some intolerable weight that was crushing the very life out of me has been lifted from my heart. I know things will be different in the future. I am going to write to my friends and ask their forgiveness as I have asked God's forgiveness!" And then Dr. Bonnell says a significant thing: "Whenever one finds an individual who has become a fount of bitterness, taunting and criticizing people, saying cruel things that wound the hearts of friends, one may be sure that he is dealing with someone who hates himself, who loathes, and despises himself, and the bitterness manifested by such a person is but the projection of his own contempt for himself."[1]

There is a world of difference between selfishness and proper self-love, between right pride and wrong pride. Wrong pride consists of a man making himself the true test of life instead of making truth the test. The selfish person is interested only in himself, wants everything for himself, feels pleasur only in taking and receiving and never giving. He looks on the world for what he can get. He must always be right.

Saroyan tells of an old man who had but one string on his cello, and he played one note on that string from morning till night, day after day, hour after hour. His patient wife finally pointed out timidly that other cellists kept changing their fingers up and down, from one position to another, all the time. He laid down his bow and looked at her with pity. "I might have expected that from you," he said. "Your hair is long but your understanding is short! Of course other players keep moving their fingers. They are trying to find the right place. I have found it!"

One of the great admirers of William E. Gladstone said of him once, "I don't object to Gladstone always having the ace of trumps up his sleeve, but I do object to his belief that Almighty God put it there!"[2]

On Loving Yourself the Right Way

This is a picture of the selfish man. He lacks interest in the needs, the hurts, the problems of others. A young man was being interviewed for a job of usher in a theater. He was asked, "What would you do in case of a fire?" "Oh, you don't have to worry about me," replied the youth, "I'll get out all right!" The selfish man feels that he is all that matters in the universe. He is like Warty the toad in Don Marquis's *Archy and Mehitabel,* who thought the world was made especially for him and said, "What has the world ever done to deserve me?" He has no respect for the dignity or the integrity of others but judges everything from the standpoint of its usefulness to him. The person who loves himself as he ought loves other people and can never be a selfish person. Meister Eckhart said, "If you love yourself properly you will love everybody else as you do yourself!" And Jesus said, "You shall love your neighbor as yourself."

Paul's word for love in 1 Corinthians 13 is *agape* which means moral love, an earnest and an unbreakable good will, an earnest desire for the best for the object of one's affection, a harmonious attitude toward all of life, a desire for creative action, friendship, brotherhood. The motive of love is to enhance, to liberate, to encourage, to make better. This definition of love certainly applies to proper love of self! It implies that you:

1. Care for your body and never abuse it or use it to gratify lust. It becomes God's temple.

2. Respect yourself. You see yourself as you are and desire to grow into what you can be.

3. Know yourself. You seek to understand your weaknesses, needs, motives, abilities, and use them fully and rightly.

4. Take responsibility for yourself. You control yourself, discipline yourself.

5. Dedicate yourself. You give yourself to the highest that you know—Jesus Christ.

Without love, life is not worth living. Smiley Blanton said in his book *Love or Perish:*

> For without love, we lose the will to live. Our mental and physical vitality is impaired, our resistance is lowered, and we succumb to illnesses that often prove fatal. We may escape actual death, but what remains is a meager and barren existence, emotionally so impoverished that we can be called only half alive![3]

Aldous Huxley said once, "Of all the worn, smudged, dog-eared words in our vocabulary, 'love' is surely the grubbiest, smelliest, slimiest. Bawled from a million pulpits, lasciviously crooned through hundreds of millions of loud speakers, it has become an outrage to good taste and decent feelings, an obscenity which one hesitates to pronounce. And yet it has to be pronounced, for, after all, love is the last word!"[4]

Proper self-love enables us to recognize and deal courageously with our sins. The selfish man says, "I haven't sinned!" Or if he admits his sin, he always has an excuse for it: grandfather, environment, great stress and strain, and so on. George Bernard Shaw said that the first prison he ever saw had inscribed on it, "Cease to do evil; learn to do well!" But the inscription was on the outside, and the men in prison couldn't see it. It should have been addressed to the self-righteous man in the street, and should have read, "All have sinned and fallen short of the glory of God!" The selfish man can always see sin in his

On Loving Yourself the Right Way 101

teacher, or roommate, or the politician, but he never or rarely admits his part in it.

A publican and a Pharisee went to the temple to pray. The Pharisee stood and boasted of his self-righteousness, his virtue, his goodness. He bragged of his good deeds and right actions. He could not see that he was a part of the wrongness of the world and that his prayer was just a recitation. The humble publican, not even daring to lift up his eyes, was the better man, and he surely had learned proper self-love, for he saw in himself his weaknesses and acknowledged them. And Jesus said that the publican, humble, penitent, went home justified. When we love ourselves as we ought, our sins are both obvious and painful. Dr. Robert Oppenheimer, one of those who worked on the first atomic explosion, quoted from another religion to sum up his feelings about what had happened: "I am become death, the shatterer of worlds!" When we love ourselves as we ought to do, we see our sins, our inability to cope with them, and realize, with the Prodigal Son, that only a loving father can ultimately save us from them. Paul asked in agony, "Who shall deliver me from the body of this death?" He answered his own question by saying, "I thank God, through our Lord Jesus Christ!"

When we love ourselves as we ought, we see ourselves as having eternal value in the sight of God. The selfish man never sees this. He is self-sufficient and never realizes his need of, or reliance upon, anyone else. William Henley belonged to this group when he said, "I am the Master of my fate, I am the Captain of my soul!"[5] Or the poet had this in mind when he said, "I fight alone, and win or sink, I need no one to set me free; I want no Jesus Christ to think, He could ever die for me!"

Football is a team effort. If one man grandstands it and tries to play quarterback, end, guard, tackle at the same time, the game is lost. But if he plays his position, does his job as a part of a team, there is always a chance to win. A man said to me once, "I have been much happier since I resigned as general manager of the universe."

To love self properly means that we see the worth of the soul. One of the most electrifying statements in the Bible is that man is made in the image of God. This makes man a person, gives him significance, and sets him apart from all else that God has made. Dr. Albert Outler in *Psychotherapy and the Christian Message* says, "If God is not, the unique self is not." It is God that makes man unique. Bishop James Armstrong says, "Man is an earthbound reflection of the divine." Man is not a thing but a human being, a person, who draws his worth from his relationship with God. The only value a human soul has is in relation to God. When we lose sight of this fact, we can mistreat our bodies and mistreat others. We lose respect for the dignity of the lives of other people. To love ourselves as we ought means that we put persons and things in proper order in our lives. God created persons to be loved and things to be used. Selfishness reverses that. Proper self-love makes us see the truth in it.

When we love ourselves as we ought, we try to discover how best we can use ourselves in life. We may not pioneer in science, or invent new machines, or discover new lands, but we can explore the abilities and possibilities that lie within us and devote them

On Loving Yourself the Right Way 103

to the service of man and God. A teacher, trying to make vivid all the new gadgets and inventions in the world, asked her class on examination, "What is in the world now that was not here fifty years ago?" One student wrote simply, "Me!" You are unique to the world. You are new, different from anything the world has ever seen. You have something to offer man and God in service through your life that has never been offered before. We thrill at the stories of Albert Schweitzer, George Washington Carver, and Wilfred Grenfell and other such people. We can't all be like them, but we can discover our own possibilities and abilities and dedicate them to the uses of God. All God wants is that we use what we have. Edwin Markham said, "There is waiting a work where only your hands can avail, and so if you falter, a chord in the music will fail!" When we love ourselves as we ought, we try to find our abilities and use them for the glory of God.

When we love ourselves properly, we accept, and are able to overcome, our handicaps, our failures, our shortcomings. In fact, we take them, accept them for what they are, and start to build a good life upon them. Many of us start out in life thinking that we are a thousand acre farm, only to come, because of some sickness, some handicap, some failure, to feel that we are a hundred-foot lot on a back alley. When Sir Harry Lauder heard the news that his son had been killed, he said, "In a time like this there are three courses open: 1. despair, sour on the world, and become a grouch; 2. try to drown sorrows in drink; 3. turn to God!" Nothing can ultimately defeat us if we love ouselves as we ought to do!

When we love ourselves properly, we become concerned with the problems of people around us. The man who has the right regard for himself, who loves himself rightly as a member of the human family, is going to try to see how many ways he can help lift the human family near to God. The selfish man sees the world only for his personal gain. The one who loves himself rightly realizes that he gains as the human race gains. Someone has said that life is like a long, narrow corridor lined on both sides with doors. The doors represent opportunities for sharing life with others. We can keep the doors closed and exists in narrow isolation, or we can open them, enter them, and become a part of a larger world of persons and interests.[6] Our business is to bring the life of God to the life of the world, and if we love ourselves as we ought, we set out to do that.

Dr. John A. Redhead, Jr., reminds us of an old legend of a father who was going away on a long trip and whose going-away present to his son was a picture of the boy himself. When the father returned the boy had starved to death because he had spent all his time looking at his own picture. Many people live like that. They live in a house of mirrors. Everywhere they turn they see only themselves. Since there are no windows in the house, they cannot see their neighbors. They starve, and they add to the misery of everyone else. A young man went to see James Russell Lowell at the turn of the century. As he thrilled at Lowell's stories about slavery and the struggle to do away with it, he exclaimed, "How I wish I could have stood at your side then!" The old man, fighter for truth that he was, walked to a window and pulled aside the curtains to reveal the smoking stacks of a great industrial plant, with wretched hovels housing

On Loving Yourself the Right Way 105

its workers, and then he asked, "What do you want more?" There are needs all around us—moral, emotional, physical needs. Some men need bread. Some need a kind word. All need God. What more chance do you want? When we love ourselves as we ought, we become concerned with the problems of the people about us, and we want to lift them nearer what God wants them to be!

How do you get a proper love for self? Jesus summed up the great commandment with "You shall love the Lord your God . . . your neighbor . . . as yourself!" We come to love ourselves properly when we love God as we ought. If we love God first, then we love ourselves in the right way and the natural result is that we will love our neighbors. People who try to love their neighbors apart from any love for God are facing an impossible task. Love for God leads naturally to right self-love, and right self-love leads to a right love for other people. Jesus revealed God to us. By surrender of our lives to God as we understand him through Jesus, we arrive at a proper self-love. In this loving relationship with God, the desire to exalt self at the expense of others, always to be at the center, to hurt and destroy all who get in the way of what we want—these go! Through this love experience with Christ our creative energies are released and enhanced, our lives are made purposeful, the ugliness of our lives disappears, we overcome and use handicaps and failures, our sins are forgiven, and we set out to use our lives to glorify God and help mankind. Love yourself the right way.

12

Ten Tests for Emotional Health

FOR MORE THAN twenty-five years I have been doing pastoral counseling. During this period I have seen thousands of people of all ages, from every strata of society, and have dealt with almost every conceivable human problem. Some I have been unable to help. Some I have helped, or at least they said so, and the results have been evident in their lives. Through the years I have learned that I know very little. I have referred many people to psychiatrists or other counselors, for I recognize my limitations. When I was in seminary, no courses were offered in pastoral care or counseling, and what I know I learned through experience, through some specialized short courses, and through extensive reading. I have come to several conclusions, but the one that seems to stand out is this: the resources available to man in the solution of his problems, through faith in God, are limitless. Often in counseling, when other therapy has failed, the resources of faith have brought healing. There is no cleavage between religion and psychiatry. Both seek the same goal—the whole person. Each may use some distinct methods, but both use in common several methods of approach.

Edward Newton had keen insight when he said: "I wish that someone would give a course in how to

Ten Tests for Emotional Health

live!" The basic wish of every person is to know how to Live. It is amazing how many ways people try to find life in its fullness. It is amazing how far short many people fall of the goal! We have come to the place in America where we seek the comfortable, easy, and often irresponsible way out of our difficulty. This accounts for the use of more than eleven billion tranquilizers in a recent year. Much of our emotional disturbance has come out of a lack of effort on our part. When things go wrong, we reach for a bottle of aspirin, an alcoholic drink, drugs, or some other tranquilizer! Our characters have been weakened, for instead of trying to learn how to live we take the comfortable, easy way out. Phillip Brooks said:

> Do not pray for easy lives.
> Pray to be a stronger man.
> Do not pray for tasks equal to your powers.
> Pray for powers equal to your tasks.[1]

We have reversed this. Wholeness is not had without effort. The course on how to live is filled with difficulties, but it is a lesson that can be learned.

What are the tests of emotional health? Here are some questions compiled from my experiences and the wisdom of several psychiatrists and other counselors with whom I have worked. They sum up the thesis of this book. The answers are left for you.

1. Do I have a purpose in life? Many a man suffers emotional depression, is agitated, substitutes loudness for depth, refuses to take responsibility simply because he has no idea where he wants to go in life. He is like the man who got on his horse and rode off in all directions! Men fail not because they are stupid

but because they are not sufficiently impassioned. Voltaire once said that some of his contemporaries were like an oven: always heating, but never cooking anything. The Apostle Paul gave the formula: "This one thing I do" (Phil. 3:3–14). What do you want out of life? Bishop Gerald Kennedy tells of an executive with Bell Laboratories who has a gadget on his desk that represents the end of the line. It is a small wooden casket, big as a cigar box, with one switch on the side. When you turn on the switch, there is a humming sound. The lid slowly opens, a hand emerges. The hand reaches down, turns off the switch, goes back into the box. The lid closes, the buzzing stops. That's all there is to it. It is a machine that switches itself off.[2] Isn't that a perfect picture of what life is for many people. No goal! No direction! No meaning! Viktor Frankl said: "In my opinion man is dominated neither by the will to pleasure, (Freud) nor by the will to power, (Adler) but by what I call the will to meaning."[3] A goal gives life direction. Do you have a clearly defined one?

2. Do I have a zest for living? Do I get up in the morning feeling as Channing Pollock said he did, that "the one divine far-off event might just happen before I sat down to breakfast?" Or, like old Rip Van Winkle, do you sleep through life's revolution? Are you satisfied with the way things are? Do you live in the past? Is there an anticipation in life that makes you stand on tiptoe?

3. Do I really like my work? We rarely break down from overwork but rather from overworry. One of the better known medical scientists said sometime ago, "One hundred percent of the fatigue of the sedentary worker, in good health, is due to emotional factors."

Ten Tests for Emotional Health 109

William James wrote: "Neither the nature nor the amount of work is accountable for the frequency and severity of our breakdowns, but their cause lies rather in those absurd feelings of hurry . . . in that breathlessness and tension, that anxiety of feature, that solicitude of result, and that lack of inner harmony and ease by which the work, with us, is apt to be accompanied."[4] A man can be destroyed emotionally by the work he does. He does not see it as creative; he sees no results of it; it does not satisfy his needs; it does not call forth the best qualities of his character. A young woman who had left college sought out a counselor. Her first words were I had a nervous breakdown and had to leave school!" The counselor worked with her for several weeks and finally reminded her of what she had said when she first came. "How would you say it now?" he asked. "I had to leave school, so I had a nervous breakdown," she replied. If a man's work is unsatisfying, he may have a nervous breakdown so that he can leave that work. How about your work? Is it really satisfying?

4. Can I face up to reality, or must I rely on drugs or others escape mechanisms to face daily life? Do I run away, or do I stand up? Aldous Huxley's book *Brave New World* was published in 1932, and it predicted the place we have given tranquilizers in our way of living. The brave new world would be one in which pain, struggle, discomfort, and effort would be eliminated. To make sure, in case some irritation came up, Huxley's world produced a drug called soma that took all the rough edges off life. He said, "We carry our virtues about with us in a bottle. Christianity without tears, that is what soma is!" Near the end of the book a savage comes from the outer

fringes of civilization. He meets the controller of the world who explains about soma. The savage protests saying, "But the tears are necessary. You get rid of them—that's just like you. Getting rid of everything unpleasant instead of learning to put up with it, you just abolish the slings and arrows. It's too easy. I don't want comfort. I want God. I want poetry. I want real danger. I want freedom. I want goodness."[5] When the controller explains that the savage would be very unhappy in any other kind of civilization than that which produced soma, the savage replies, 'I claim the right to be unhappy!" We have weakened our characters by running and by using liquor and drugs to dull our senses. Can you face up to life?

5. Can I frankly admit my weaknesses as well as my strengths? How many people are so unstable that they can never admit that they might just once be wrong, or mistaken. A woman said once that neither she nor any member of her family would ever get on their knees and say, "Have mercy upon me, O Lord. According to the multitude of thy tender mercies blot out my transgressions." They hadn't committed any! The people of St. George's, Edinburgh, still talk about that memorable day when Alexander Whyte leaned over his pulpit during a service and said, "This week I met the wickedest man in Edinburgh. And his name is Alexander Whyte." If we are to be whole, we must be willing to face our weaknesses as well as our strengths, our failures as well as our successes.

6. Do I really love someone else? Do I have a friend or friends in whom I may confide? Do I trust people reasonably? Am I concerned with others? Joshua Liebman wrote: "Next to bread, love is the food

Ten Tests for Emotional Health   111

that all mortals most hunger for; it is the essential vitamin of the soul." Actually, more people perish for lack of love than for lack of bread. We need to develop the power to love even the unlovely. The more we try to do this, the greater becomes our capacity to receive love and give love. Maurice Maeterlinck has a beautiful, wistful line in "The Treasure of the Humble": "There is no soul that does not respond to love, for the soul of man is a guest that has gone hungry these centuries back." How important it is that we learn to love another for himself, with a positive, constructive, self-forgetting love, love that is good will, friendship, brotherhood. We must learn to live beyond, outside ourselves to be whole.

7. Do I seriously try to correct my faults? Almost every character or personality defect has its origin in self-centeredness. One day my seventh-grade teacher, Miss Carrie Mae Patterson, went to the blackboard and wrote the word selfishness. Then she divided the word into three parts: self, ish, ness. "Note," she said, "that the first letter of each of these parts makes the word *sin*." Self is enthroned, protected, worshiped. We must have our own way. The psalmist cried out, "Who can understand his errors? Cleanse thou me from secret faults." We must make every effort to understand what our faults are. "Know thyself" includes knowing our faults for what they are An honest seeking to know our failures and shortcomings and then to be rid of them is essential to emotional health.

8. Am I a happy person? Is my general outlook on life one of optimism and hope? All of us have problems. Lately in every meeting I attend half the time

seems to be spent listing problems. This gets depressing. Of course, we cannot be blind to problems. But we can open our eyes to life's possibilities. Do I generally have a pleasant outlook toward life? Do I try to find the bright side of life, life with its possibilities rather than its problems?

9. Do I know how to worry correctly? A man told me the other day that he had so many worries that if anything else happened it would be two weeks before he could worry about it. There are many causes and kinds of worry, but there is a difference between legitimate planning and senseless worry! I have a card on my desk that says, "God grant me the serenity to accept the things I cannot change; the courage to change the things I can; and the wisdom to know the difference." Don't be "a self-centered little clod of ailments and grievances, complaining that the world will not devote itself to making you happy." (G. B. Shaw) Learn to worry correctly.

10. Do I have and practice a vital religious faith? Dr. John D. Campbell, in his paper "Psychiatry and Religion," says, "Religion encourages a sane, regular, temperate, and purposeful life, the very practices which produce the greatest peace of mind."[6] The medical profession is hailing new drugs almost every day. Some time ago there was a new drug from India called Rawolfia. There is, however, another "R" that provides more healing and wholeness than all drugs together—religion. It produces more serenity than phenobarbital. It doesn't lull us to sleep. It doesn't stupefy like morphine or liquor. It doesn't delude like LSD. It doesn't require a prescription. Research reveals there is a lower incidence of ulcer, divorce, and juvenile delinquency among men and women of

Ten Tests for Emotional Health

genuine faith, those who really believe and practice. Man is not created to be Atlas. He cannot bear the weight of the world or of his own life for that matter. But teamed with God, the resources available to man through faith are limitless.

Notes

CHAPTER 1

1. Paul Tournier, *The Person Reborn* (New York: Harper & Row, 1966), p. 75.
2. Leslie Weatherhead, *Psychology, Religion, and Healing* (Nashville: Abingdon, 1951), p. 37.
3. Paul Tillich, *The New Being* (New York: Charles Scribner's Sons, 1955), p. 9.
4. Weatherhead, *Psychology, Religion, and Healing*, p. 80.
5. Paul Tillich, *Pastoral Psychology,* June 1958, p. 8.

CHAPTER 2

1. Russell L. Dicks, *Toward Health and Wholeness* (New York: Macmillan, 1960), p. 155.
2. Quoted in Norman Vincent Peale, "Faith Is the Answer," *Pulpit Digest,* March 1957.
3. John S. Bonnell, *No Escape from Life* (New York: Harper & Row, 1958), p. 130.
4. Quoted in Agnes Sanford, *The Healing Light* (St. Paul: Macalester Park, 1947), p. 20.
5. Quoted in Willis W. Willard, Jr., "What Faith Can Do," *Pulpit Digest,* March 1957.

6. Weatherhead, *Psychology, Religion, and Healing*, p. 432.

Chapter 3

1. E. S. Hocking, *Human Nature and Its Remaking*, quoted by Ralph Sockman in *Pulpit Digest*, February, 1948.
2. William James, *The Varieties of Religious Experience* (London: Longmans Green, 1917).

Chapter 4

1. John S. Bonnell, *Do You Want to Be Healed?* (New York: Harper & Row, 1968), p. 93.
2. T. S. Eliot, "The Cocktail Party," *The Complete Poems and Plays of T. S. Eliot* (New York: Harcourt Brace, 1952).
3. E. Stanley Jones, *How to Be a Transformed Person*, quoted by John A. Redhead, *Learning to Have Faith* (Nashville: Abingdon, 1955), p. 46.
4. John Bunyan, *Complete Works* (Philadelphia: Bradley Garretson and Company, 1881), p. 104.

Chapter 5

1. E. Stanley Jones, *The Way to Power and Poise* (Nashville: Abingdon, 1949), p. vii, used by permission.
2. Eric W. Barnes, *The Man Who Lived Twice* (New York: Charles Scribner's Sons, 1956).

Chapter 6

1. A. E. Housman, *Last Poems* (New York: Henry Holt, 1922).
2. William L. Stidger, *Human Interest Stories in Christian Stewardship* (Chicago: The Methodist Church, Board of Lay Activities, 1947), p. 55.

Chapter 7

1. Halford E. Luccock, *Never Forget to Live* (Nashville: Abingdon, 1956), p. 125.
2. Ralph W. Sockman, from sermon broadcast 19 June 1960, published by National Council of Churches, National Radio Pulpit.
3. Robert E. Luccock, *If God Be for Us* (New York: Harper & Row, 1954), p. 49.
4. Elton Trueblood, *The New Man for Our Time* (New York: Harper & Row, 1970), p. 79.
5. John Donne, *Devotions upon Emergent Occasions* (Ann Arbor: University of Michigan Press, 1959), p. 109.

Chapter 8

1. Viktor Frankl, *Man's Search for Meaning* (New York: Washington Square Press, 1963), p. 104.
2. John Masefield *Poems* (London: William Heinemann, Ltd., 1923), p. 73.

Chapter 9

1. Clarence E. Macartney, *Macartney's Illustrations* (Nashville: Abingdon, 1945), p. 28.
2. John S. Bonnell, *No Escape from Life*, p. 93.
3. From an address by Bishop H. Clifford Northcutt at the 1960 General Conference of The Methodist Church.

Chapter 10

1. From a sermon preached by Ralph Sockman, 13 January 1957, published by National Council of The Church of Christ in America.
2. Rudyard Kipling, "If," *Masterpieces of Religious Verse* (New York: Harper & Row, 1948), p. 279.

3. Quoted in E. Stanley Jones, *Conversion* (Nashville: Abingdon, 1949), p. 134.
4. Quoted in *Masterpieces of Religious Verse*, p. 605.
5. John Masefield, *The Trial of Jesus* (New York: Macmillan, 1925), p. 111.

Chapter 11

1. Bonnell, *Do You Want to Be Healed?* p. 97.
2. Gerald Kennedy, *A Reader's Notebook* (New York: Harper & Row, 1953), p. 228.
3. Smiley Blanton, *Love or Perish* (New York: Simon and Schuster, 1956), p. 4.
4. Aldous Huxley, *Tomorrow and Tomorrow and Tomorrow* (London: Chatto and Windus, Ltd., 1952).
5. William E. Henley, *Poems* (London: David Nutt, 1898), p. 119.
6. James Armstrong, *The Journey That Men Make* (Nashville: Abingdon, 1969), p. 146.

Chapter 12

1. Quoted in Bonnell, *No Escape from Life*.
2. Gerald Kennedy, *The Parables* (New York: Harper & Row, 1960), p. 38.
3. Viktor E. Frankl, *Man's Search for Meaning* (New York: Washington Square Press, 1963).
4. Quoted by Bonnell, *No Escape from Life*, p. 145.
5. Aldous Huxley, *Brave New World* (New York: Harper & Row, 1960), p. 183.
6. John D. Campbell, "Psychiatry and Religion," *Journal of the Medical Association of Georgia*, August 1949.

About The Author

Dr. Cecil Myers is senior minister of the Peachtree Road United Methodist Church in Atlanta, Georgia, having served over thirty years in various pastorates in that same state. In addition to his role as counselor-minister, Dr. Myers serves in leadership positions in numerous denominational and civic organizations. He is a well-known after-dinner speaker, much in demand on college campuses.

Dr. Myers completed his education at the University of Chattanooga and Candler School of Theology, Emory University. He received his D.D. from LaGrange College.

Presently Dr. Myers serves as a member of the World Family Life Committee of the United Methodist Church and as clergy leader of the North Georgia Delegation to the 1976 General United Methodist Conference. He has contributed numerous articles to various magazines and has published several books including *Happiness Is Still Homemade* and *You Can Be More Than You Are*.